ANDY LEWIS was born in Bedminster Down, Bristol in 1953. He attended the local secondary school before completing an apprenticeship as an electrical fitter. For the last twenty-five years he has worked for Bristol Water, just a few hundred yards from the site of the former Bedminster Down Boys' Club.

Known throughout South Bristol by his nickname, Lou, he is married with four children and a growing number of grandchildren.

Girls Not Allowed:
A History of Bedminster Down Boys' Club

Andy Lewis

SilverWood

Published in 2014 by SilverWood Books

SilverWood Books Ltd
30 Queen Charlotte Street, Bristol, BS1 4HJ
www.silverwoodbooks.co.uk

ISBN 978-1-78132-235-2

British Library Cataloguing in Publication Data
A CIP catalogue record for this book is available from
the British Library

Set in Sabon by SilverWood Books
Printed by Imprint Digital on responsibly sourced paper

To the thousands of you that were part of this club's rich history, you will all forever be part of something that was truly special.

And most importantly to my wife Jayne, and children, Emma, Kate, Ben & Sam. So much of our inspiration comes from those we love.

Contents

Acknowledgements

I would like to place on record my personal thanks to the following for their support and encouragement during this whole project: Nick and Ali, Dave and Diane, Paul and Deb, Bratch, Barry, Di Toft, my brother Martin, Helen Hart and everyone at SilverWood Books.

To Lorna Rollings for providing the author photograph and Pete Moreman for providing additional photographs from the Bedminster Down Boys' Club archive.

Foreword

If you live in South Bristol you would know of Bedminster Down Boys' Club – such was its mighty presence.

If you were standing within 50 yards of Andy Lewis you would know it – such is his mighty presence.

This book is a marvellous memoir of Andy Lou's sweet and sour time at Bemmy Down Boys' Club – from watching the club being built in 1964 to its demolition in 2006.

Like thousands of boys and young men, he enjoyed the wonderful experiences and opportunities that membership of a traditional boys' club could bring. Like a fair number, he stayed on to volunteer his help. However, like very few, that help lasted over thirty years (deserving of a Gold Certificate in the glory days of the National Association of Boys' Clubs).

Like no one else, Andy ensured the survival of the Club through a series of dramas and crises.

In the end, even he could not save the Club building and Club membership from the prejudices, jealousies and resentments of the authorities and, most depressingly, the very organisation that had the duty and finance to support us.

What Andy could do, though, was preserve the memory of Bedminster Down Boys' Club.

This book is part of a project that, with Andy's characteristic determination and typical 'get off your ass and do it' attitude, will embrace volumes of photographs, press reports, videos, documents and the memories of the countless people whose lives were touched by a uniquely brilliant organisation.

I feel privileged to have been given the opportunity to read Andy's first drafts of his book and honoured to have been asked to write this foreword. It also gives me the opportunity to correct some glaring omissions from Andy's script: "Shoot me!", "Bloody stroll on!!" and "All NBC (members of the erstwhile National Boys' Club) are tosspots!!!"

Dave Scarborough
Bedminster Down Boys' Club Treasurer 1971 – 2004.

Preface

I'm still not sure whether to start at the beginning or to start at the end. For those who were there at the end I have no doubt that the impact was huge, for those who were there at the start but not the end – well, they will have another view on it. However, for those of us that lived the whole story, well, most of it anyway, our story will be more complete. So, as somebody who falls into that category, here is my story about my time at Bedminster Down Boys' Club (BDBC).

It was Wednesday 16 June 2004, the day when this local youth facility that had served the area of Bedminster Down for over sixty years would close its doors for good. There was a strange atmosphere throughout the club that night. I'm not sure that many of the members who were in were aware of what was actually happening. Oh yes, they knew the club was closing, but to have an understanding of the impact of that closure – well, I'm not so sure about that.

Some old boys had called in, and there were many of the present staff group – which, at the time, didn't amount to many. The Evening Post photographer had arrived and was busy taking those historic photos that would be seen in the local paper the following day. I found myself gazing at the wall of the main club area, I can't recall now what I was gazing at, but for a moment in time my mind wandered back – back to those heady days when I was a member. I could feel a deep sadness creep over my whole body and my eyes watered. I felt a hand on my shoulder and a voice said, "Are you okay, Lou?" (Lou had been my nickname for as long as I could remember. I'm sure there are many members who went through their whole time at the Club not actually knowing what my real name was) I turned and looked into the eyes of the young man behind me – I struggled to speak, so just said, "No, Pickle, I'm not". Pickle, aka Mark Williams, was one of the few young helpers left at the end. Like most of those who had gone before him, he had started off as a junior member many years earlier. This was the end of the road; no more would this great institution serve the community that had supported it since 1941.

1

New Beginnings, New Hopes and Aspirations

Knowing where to start is difficult, as I sit here writing this some nine years after the closure. We tend, I suppose, to go through life dealing with the issues it throws at us as we go. It's probably only on reflection that we understand the impact that those events have had on us.

It's probably safe to say that my time at the Bedminster Down Boys' Club has been the single biggest influence on my life, and still is. It made me the person that I am. It's contributed to any successes and played its part in those things that weren't so successful – or failures as it's easier to understand – I still don't dig this PC rubbish.

Well here goes, here's my story...

In September 1941, three lads left Marksbury Road Lads' Club to form a new club on Bedminster Down. It was called Mark III Lads' Club, Bedminster Down. The club opened on Thursday 11 September 1941, at Bedminster Down Junior School in Cheddar Grove.

The membership of the new club saw highs and lows during the years that followed, not surprising as we were in the middle of the Second World War. The leader at that time, Reg Hewitt, resigned in 1947 and the membership numbers plummeted to five in 1950. In 1953, Stephen Kew was appointed as chairman and in 1958, the club moved to new premises, a pavilion at Langford Road. In November 1960, Mr N Durbin was appointed as leader and the following year the club announced plans to build new premises at a cost of £6,000.

It was 1964, and I was eleven years old. Outside school, activities fell into very few categories in those days, with only the uniformed organisations or a couple of youth clubs that existed. Both categories were normally linked to the same institution – the Church.

Being brought up on Bedminster Down, you could fall into one of two groups: the 170th St Oswald's Cub and Scout Group, attached to St Oswald's Church in Cheddar Grove; or, as I did with my two older brothers, the 266th Zion Methodist Cub and Scout Group, attached to the Zion Methodist Church on Bishopsworth Road. There was intense rivalry between the two groups, as intense as the rivalry between the supporters of the red and blue halves of our city. Both churches had youth clubs, mainly attended by those older youths that went to the relevant churches. Both youth clubs met in church halls adjacent to the churches.

There is no doubt that both uniformed groups were strong, well-run organisations. I joined the Cubs at the age of eight and engaged myself in the activities it could provide. The Scoutmaster was John Blackmore, and his wife, Joyce, was in charge of the Cubs – Akela. We met on Wednesday nights at the Sunday School Hall, next to the church.

We didn't travel very far in those days. I walked to the local Infants and Junior Schools in Cheddar Grove, and walked to Ashton Gate to watch my beloved Bristol City (well, it was beloved then). South Bristol had a few uniformed groups. The 9th Headley Park, which met at the bottom of Headley Lane, the 14th Withywood, and the 60th Bristol Congregational in Grange Road, to name a few. There was also a group in Hartcliffe, and it was playing in a Scout football competition that I first met Mike and Bob Sullivan, who both excelled in the Bristol Amateur Football circuit years later.

The movement from Cubs to Scouts happened when you were eleven, and involved you being thrown over a rope by your colleagues. A bit of a challenge as I wasn't the lightest of Cubs! However, a Scout I became – following in the steps of my old mate Barry Lovell, who had made the move months earlier. So, three Lewis boys in the same Scout troop, and I was the youngest. It was May 1964.

At the same time as the shenanigans of me being thrown over a rope in the Zion Church Hall were occurring, an even bigger event was happening just a short walk along Brunel Road. Builders were completing the erection of a new building, next door to the Ex-Servicemen's Club in Winford Grove. Why they called it a club in those days mystified me, as it was nothing more than a Nissen hut. A strange building it was, and I used to get a good look at it when the school football team played at home. As I stated, I went to Cheddar Grove Infants and Junior Schools. If you played for the school football team you had the pleasure of carrying the football posts from the school, up Cheddar Grove, along Winford Grove, across the grass in front of Brunel Road, then across the main A38 on to the football pitch. It seemed to take ages, with four of us struggling to carry a cross bar – then you would make the same journey back, often in the wet, and often after losing the bloody game.

This new building being erected was going to be a boys' club – what that meant at the time I had no idea. It wasn't something I gave much thought to – you had to be fourteen to join anyway, and that seemed a long time away.

Quite why the following events happened, I am not sure. My father was a carpenter, and I know that my brother, Martin, joined the new boys' club in September 1965. What I do know is that Dad would disappear to this boys' club some evenings doing woodwork. Anyway, for some strange reason I was told they were having a couple of guests for Sunday lunch – two people from the club. They turned out to be Steve Long (the leader) and Dave Phillips (described as his assistant).

My mother always put on a good lunch, basic but good. There would be plenty of vegetables, a joint of meat (based on what father had earned), and a home-made pudding. Christ, could these two blokes eat – and talk. To make things worse, the one called Dave liked his sherry, and he knocked back nearly a full bottle. When I eventually joined the club I found that Dave had inherited the name Waffler – easy to see why.

Between the eating, drinking and incessant talking, I managed to get a question in to our two visitors. "Why is this new club of yours not open for people of my age?" "It will be," came the response – "We are planning a junior section soon. Why don't you come up with your dad when he's working and have a look around?" And that was the start of it.

It was eventually November 1966 when I joined the junior section of Bedminster Down Boys' Club.

I had taken them up on the offer that Sunday, and used to walk up to the club on the nights Dad was up there. He was building bench seats in the changing rooms, and I would busy myself with a brush sweeping up after him. When the work was finished for the night, the workers, which were mostly helpers or very senior members, would go into the gym and play three-a-side football. I felt very privileged. It was the first time that I noticed that this somewhat strange leader, who was called Longer, had a very pronounced limp. However, he seemed to ignore this disability completely when in the gym. He obviously loved football – something that would be questioned many times over the forthcoming years.

The junior section opened in 1966, and you had to be thirteen years of age. One problem – it only took place on a Thursday night, and that was the evening I went to Scouts. No matter how much you cut it, you can't be in two separate places at the same time, even if they are only 400 metres apart. I was desperate to join the club, but actually enjoyed Scouts immensely. Mum and Dad were of no support whatsoever – "Up to you," they said, "but you need to speak to John, the Scout leader, if you are going to leave." John Blackmore lived just along the road from us, in Brooklyn Road. He was a wonderful man, who gave most of his life to the 266th. I explained the problem, he didn't want me to leave, but wished me well – "If it doesn't work out, come back," he said. So I left, leaving my old mate Barry behind. Suddenly, new frontiers had opened up for the young males in Bedminster Down, and many of them put away their neckerchiefs and woggles for the last time. While the 170th and the 266th Scout troops have since disappeared, there is still a vibrant uniformed organisation on Bedminster Down some forty years later. Blenheim Venture Scouts provide a wonderful service to the young people of Bedminster Down.

And so eventually, some two years after the place opened, I had my name on the subs list at BDBC.

The new club building in 1964

2

Fried Onions and Football

By this time, I knew many of the helpers at the club and some of the more senior members. The likes of Longer, Waffler, Esky, Sherman, and Our Rog, were now household names for me as a result of my night-time working party escapades. However, it was a different face that approached me during one of the first Thursday nights I enjoyed at the club. "Do you fancy a game of table tennis?" a voice asked. Attending Bedminster Down School, and having an older brother there at the same time, meant I knew most of the males that attended the local education establishment. However, this was a face that I didn't recognise, and as it turned out – it was a face that I would see regularly at the club over the next thirty-eight years, and someone who became a stalwart of the organisation – Dave Scarborough, or as we all began to call him Scarby.

In the first two years since it opened in its new premises, the club had established a very strong parent support group. Adults were involved in running a huge range of sports teams, and very importantly were fully running the club canteen. The ladies group was in full swing. Senior nights were firmly established three nights a week on a Monday, Wednesday and Friday, a change from the Monday, Thursday and Friday when it opened. Poor attendance on a Thursday allowed the newly established juniors to start, and a new senior night opened on a Wednesday.

The three senior nights all had their established ladies

behind the canteen: June Sandy and Audrey Thompson (who doubled up as the club cleaners during the day), Olive Sollars and Bina Groves, and Ada Hurditch. At some point, Rose Lewis (yes, Mother) and Bett Hall replaced Ada on a Friday. Each pair had their own speciality, salad rolls one night, toast another, and hotdogs on a Friday (replacing Ada's bacon rolls). Now, the hotdogs on a Friday presented a particular problem in the Lewis household, as my father hated the smell of fried onions. The demand for hotdogs was so big, Bett and Rose decided they would have to cook them at home in advance, and then transport them to the club on a Friday night. They took it in turns doing the onions. The sausages were provided free by Arthur Cox, who ran the butcher's at the bottom of Bedminster Down Road.

These were the great days before supermarkets. Home produce was delivered direct to your door by the milkman, the butcher, the fishmonger, and, of course, the coalman. Arthur Cox was the local butcher, his brother Stan drove a small white van around the area, and your meat was carved up in front of you from the back of the van. My dad had been working for W.J. Kew Builders since he was de-mobbed, for many years as a general foreman. The story goes that he was thinking of going self-employed, but it was a big decision with four children to support. One day Arthur Cox walked up to him and put £50 in his hand – "Go, buy yourself a van, you're going self-employed. At some point in the future, I will ask for my £50 back, make sure you got it." Dad told me that he put the £50 away from his first jobs – it was five years later that Arthur casually said, "Can I have my £50?" Dad didn't disappoint. When Arthur knew the old man was helping out at the club, the sausages were provided for free. That arrangement continued for many years, the community of Bedminster Down was helping its own.

Anyway – Royston Lewis hated the smell of onions, so poor Rose would hastily fry them all up, cover them in tin foil, and then spend hours trying to get rid of the smell. How often Bett would cook the onions I am not sure – not often enough as far as Royston was concerned. Bett Hall was the wife of Bill Hall. Bill was the manager of the under-18s football team when I first became a member of the club.

In the years prior to opening in the new building, Bedminster Down Lads' Club, as it was called then, had been very successful on the football pitch. Just prior to the new building opening in August 1964, the under-18s team, which operated from the club's then-current premises in Langford Road, a pavilion affectionately known as the Green Hut, won the GFA Minor Cup, defeating Avon Athletic 4 – 3, after extra time. A year later, in April 1965, the then under-18s side beat Kingswood Youth Centre 2 – 1, to win the GYFA Under-18 Cup. This game was memorable for two reasons. First, it was played at Ashton Gate, the home of Bristol City Football Club. Second, the captain of the side, Keith Swift, was carried off with a broken leg, and we played a significant part of the game with only ten men. I was lucky enough to watch that game, kitted out with home-made rosettes made by the ladies' group. All the team were locals. Along with Keith, there was Dave Laken, Andy Venn, Dave 'Oscar' O'Shea, and many more. Some thirty-nine years later, some of the players joined us for the Final Dinner, they were the earliest members I remember, and I was honoured they joined us that night.

Talking to Andy Venn just recently, he reflected on that period of time back when the club opened in Winford Grove: "We were a successful football team, and when the club opened we had visions of being able to use the facilities for training. Steve didn't really welcome us with open-arms – after all, most of us were working. Most of us left after that victory, going into adult football." Steve was just twenty-three years old when he was appointed the full-time leader of Bedminster Down Boys' Club. This was probably the first occasion when he clashed with his older members, but it wouldn't be the last, and it wouldn't be the last time that a football team would get into trouble with the club leader. In fact, the next clash was just around the corner.

Bill Hall lived in Ilchester Crescent. He had taken over as the manager of the under-17s football team, and took them to the Cup Final in April 1966, where they drew 1 – 1 with Eagle House Youth Club at Harvey's Ground, in Whitchurch. This was no ordinary football team, and certainly one that you would recognise in this day and age. They had their own female support group. Not young, attractive WAGS hanging on to every word their boyfriends uttered, these were more mature females, but every much as venomous as the modern day WAGS – these were the mums.

The mums would be there at every home game, and travel to the away games – sometimes by coach! They were easily recognisable, as most of them were involved in the club in some way – they were the cleaners, the canteen staff, the ladies

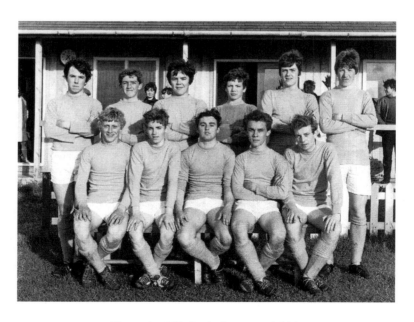

The under 18's football team in 1966

24

doing the sorting and selling at the jumble sales, and the ladies that made the cakes at the Christmas Fayre. There was Stella, June, Audrey, Margaret, Bett, to name but a few. The same territorial or tribal mentality existed between the teams representing boys' clubs in South Bristol, as it did with the uniformed organisations – but more so.

As the teams moved up from under-17s to under-18s, an increase in testosterone went with them. Games between us and those from Hartcliffe Boys' Club and Eagle House Youth Club were often tense affairs, in more ways than one. At one home game with Hartcliffe Boys Club, many of the players from Eagle House suddenly arrived as spectators. They didn't have a fixture themselves, and as the outcome of the game significantly affected them they decided to turn up to watch. As the tensions rose on the pitch, so they rose off the pitch. Banter turned to abuse, and suddenly a number of the mums launched into some of the Eagle House players with their umbrellas – it was spectacular.

The then under-18s finished their time at the club with a 2 – 1 victory against Hartcliffe BC in the Federation of Boys' Clubs Cup Final at Eastville Stadium on 26 April 1967. They were a great team, with some great players – probably one of the best football teams the club has produced. There was Mike Sollars, Steve Coles, Brian Hall, Graham Packer, Ian Pallent, Bob Cook, Dave Rogers, Barry Kew and Michael 'Joe' Thompson. But successful football teams, particularly in older age groups, for the most part, had a particularly strained relationship with the leader over the years. Steve loved sport, the myth that he hated all things football, was unfair. What he did hate was what football had become. He was brought up in an era of Finney, Lawton, Matthews...football purists. In later years, it was the great Brian Clough that Steve would hold up as his hero and he spent many years attempting to lure him to BDBC to be a guest at one of our Open Nights – unsuccessfully, I might add. I was never sure if Steve was an admirer of Clough as a footballer, a football manager, or simply for the person that he was. After all, Cloughie was a controversial character, he was self-opinionated, a critic of the establishment, and supremely confident in his own ability – very much his own man. It wouldn't be very much off the mark to say that there were certain similarities between both of them!

Steve disliked the elevated status that footballers believed they had, at any level. Interestingly, the Bristol Federation of Boys' Clubs (BFBC) had started their football league to provide an opportunity for those less able footballers, who wouldn't get a game elsewhere. The problem was that there were very few boys' football teams in those days. So, if you wanted to play the nation's national sport – your local boys' club could provide the answer.

On some occasions, you had enough players in an age group to have two teams. Unfortunately, the BFBC didn't always run leagues in the age groups you wanted. It might be under-16s and under-14s one year, and then under-15s and under-14s the next. For me, it didn't really matter – we were hammered every week no matter what the age group was. The other interesting thing was that you often played against players that you had played against at school level. And at school level, it was the same players that represented their schools at rugby, football and cricket – some we all got to know very well. Mutual dislike could easily be transferred through each school sport every year!

Unfortunately for me, there were some very gifted footballers at my age group – and most of them played for other teams. Teams like Hillfields Youth Club, Speedwell Boys' Club, Eagle House Youth Club, and Bedminster YMCA must have looked on playing BDBC with relish during 1968. We, or me in particular as goalkeeper, used to ship goals for a pastime. I remember losing 17 – 1, 21 – 0 and 19 – 0 in three consecutive games. Geoff Patch, who played for Eagle House, seemed to score at will against us. However, unlike many of the other gifted players that plagued my Saturday afternoon, Geoff wasn't arrogant or bullish – he was a good 'un. Transport to away games wasn't always available. On some occasions, we went by bus, and on other occasions we walked – I can't see many of today's youngsters doing that! Referees were a luxury; we always seemed to have one for our home games – but never for the away ones. We travelled to play Broad Plain Boys' Club one Saturday. We caught a bus into Bedminster, and then another one up to Knowle. The referee was a lunatic, with extremely long hair and earrings (male body piercing was not widespread then). Within the first ten minutes, he threatened to give Mervyn Cook a 'fucking good kicking'. We played the rest of the game in fear of our lives, were chased off the ground by the spectators at the end, after losing – and then had to get two buses home. Sheer joy!

Football was a must in the club's activity programme over the years. However, accommodating the needs for training and providing adult helpers to run the teams could prove to be difficult at times. Many voluntary staff gave up their Saturdays to run football teams with varying degrees of success, although that depends how you measure success. There were successes and failures at all levels. There were good managers and some not so good, including some rank bad ones. For some managers, it was about winning, for others it was for the sheer pleasure of providing an opportunity for those boys. Some of the managers were the fathers of members; others were purely members of the voluntary staff team. Some of them weren't even keen on the game. Steve was obsessed with the way the teams were run. Players had to train to play, they couldn't owe any subs, they had to do their bit in Club Week. We had all the rules, and all the arguments that went with them.

The club year would always start with a discussion about the Club Programme, and that's when the debates would start. It was obvious that some of the football teams on occasions had arranged a pre-meeting, so they could attend the meeting about the programme in a position to influence the debate. The night, the time – it was all up for grabs. You had to be on your toes when the teams were posted on the notice board, had the players been at training, had they paid their subs, and later in the year – had they raised the required amount for Club Week?

It was in 1968 that Roy James first appeared on the scene, it was all a bit of a surprise at the time. We had two under-15s teams, but one of the teams was made up of mainly under-14s. We arrived for our Wednesday night training session as usual, and were promptly told that this new man would be taking training from now on. Now, the story goes that Roy was working for Social Services at the time, and knew Dave Phillips, as they were both Child Care Officers. He was looking to make a career change and become a teacher, and had been roped in to do some coaching at BDBC. Unfortunately, in his introduction, Steve had made the mistake of telling all assembled that Roy was a former professional at Bristol Rovers Football Club and at one stage was tipped to replace the great Geoff Bradford. That provided the cue for most of us in the under-15s team to spend the next few weeks trying to kick the shit out of him in the gym. God knows what he must have thought. In contrast, the other team, made up of a lot of younger players, were all sweetness and light. The younger team was captained by John Tanner, and it was John that became the innocent target of retribution some twelve months later.

John was a good player, and he had a very likeable disposition. Steve did have his favourites, he always would. You couldn't put a finger on why it would be this member, or that member – but he had them. I certainly wasn't one of his favourites back then – but that's another story. Both the under-15s teams were being hammered every week – it was bleak. At the end of the 1968-69 season, The Evening Post decided to hold a competition for the Junior Harry Bamford Trophy.

Steve, in conjunction with Roy, had decided to nominate

John for the award – and he won. The trophy was presented at Ashton Gate with much pomp and ceremony on 28 April 1969. It would be fair to say that many of the players in the same age group weren't best pleased. Looking back, that was pretty understandable – John had been singled out as a role model above all the other players in the age group. His reward was a trophy and a good kicking the next time he went in the gym. After a very challenging start, including a period when he nearly wrapped it in, Roy spent years coaching the football teams at the club. When he retired from football in May 1988, we managed to arrange a surprise farewell match for him at the club. He turned up at the club without knowing that many of the players he trained over the years had assembled to pay tribute to him. It was a lovely warm summer's evening in May, and some of the finest footballers that the club had produced under Roy lined up to pay their respects. I still wonder, to this day, how we pulled it off without him knowing. There were twenty-six old boys, six current members at that time, plus Roy and Micky Slocombe, another ex-Bristol Rovers player from the same period as Roy. The kit was provided courtesy of

Roy James' retirement, May 1988

Highridge United, a club that was full of former boys' club members. Okay, I admit that some of us struggled to get into the shirts but the game itself was played in good spirit, and no-quarter was given. Using my executive powers I managed to get twenty minutes on the pitch – and I will always be grateful to all those players who took part, and to Jim Smith (manager of Queens Park Rangers) who gave permission for Nicky Johns to play. The evening itself became more poignant as a result of Roy's sudden death two years later. Most of the players who played that evening once again assembled to pay their respects to Roy, this time at All Saints Church, Long Ashton.

BDBC did produce some talented footballers over the years. Alex Ball and Mike Trought had fairly short professional careers with Bristol City and Bristol Rovers respectively, while Nicky Johns, probably our greatest sporting export, played just under 400 games professionally, including 288 for Charlton Athletic between 1979 – 1988. On occasions, you would have a good football cohort that would go through their time at the club with a great deal of success. One of those teams was managed by Our Rog Grimley, and consisted of the likes of Paul Thompson, Mark Johns, Mark Pratten, Dave Brace, Gary Marks, Chris Bisp and Barry Enever. Roger was a great character but I will never be convinced that he influenced the tactics on the field of play for that team! What he did do was ensure they all knew what their responsibilities were towards the club, they were not only successful they were a great group of lads.

Both Marks (Johns and Pratten) came from Withywood (a large council estate to the south of Bedminster Down) – they were talented footballers and Mark Johns, Nicky's brother, played a couple of times for the Rovers. There emerged some strong cohorts of footballers from Withywood during the 1970s – Andy Mathias, or God, as I nicknamed him years later (which was more to do with his own evaluation of his ability than anything else), Alan Tucker, the Blakeleys (Steve and Kevin), Rob Meecham, Paul Jenkins, Mike Cains and Colin Bullock all came from the Woods. Andy Mathias or Mac was a character – and a good footballer. Andy lived locally, moving to Tyntesfield Road from Withywood, but attended Withywood School and wore the green, black and white sports shirt of Withywood School with pride – as all Withywood lads did. We actually played in the same football team at one stage – Bishopsworth United Sunday. I was at the end of my career as a local parks footballer, and Andy was probably still only fifteen or sixteen years of age. On the football pitch, he was gifted and just a wee bit arrogant. Unfortunately for most of the teams we played against at that stage, they weren't good enough to get anywhere near him – so they couldn't kick him! Many years later, I was honoured that Andy asked me to be godfather to his daughter, Hannah. I think Andy would agree that the club had a major impact on his life.

Controversy is never far away from football, regardless of the level or standard involved. It wasn't any different at the club. In 1979, for instance, club helper, Ted Longford, suspended every player in his team for two weeks due to disciplinary issues. Ted had taken his under-16s team into senior football and this was their second season at that level. Ted probably wasn't the best example of your ideal club football team manager but he had the guts to take decisive action when it was required. I can think of some talented footballers who went through the club always thinking that they didn't necessarily need to conform to the same rules as everyone else. And then you have those who completely engrossed themselves in the club's ethos and culture.

Russ Cooper had plenty of success with football teams during his tenure as club leader. Whether it was purely down to the cohort of members at that time, or whether in part to Russ being keen to develop sporting excellence, I wouldn't know. Regardless, he didn't surrender any principles of club membership along the way – and the club produced some very good teams during that period. Of course, the likes of Alex Ball and Mike Trought will be the prominent ones of the period due to their ventures into the professional game – however, there were many more that played in a high standard of football at amateur level. What was also interesting were the family connections between some of them. Mike Trought's father was Dave Trought, another accomplished player and former club member. Dave's brother was Jeff, a former member also and a school teammate of mine who played at a high standard. Both James and Ross Hickery were decent footballers, but followed their father Kevin into local rugby. Kevin was an all-round sportsman but excelled as a scrum-half in Imperial First XV for years. Kevin has legendary status in the club's history.

Although only three members made it to the professional stage there are many others that played at the highest level at an amateur level, and have probably earned a few shillings at the same time.

In addition to the standard eleven-a-side Saturday League

The under 16's football team 1996 – 97

format there were also five-a-side, six-a-side, junior section teams, and a range of teams from under-12s through to under-18s, and even at one point a senior team, yes adults. The five-a-side Federation competition nearly always took place at those clubs that were lucky to have an outside court. For us, at BDBC, that normally meant a visit to Hartcliffe Boys' Club or Eagle House Youth Club. The interesting thing about these games was that while Saturday afternoon matches were often watched by a handful of spectators (if that), the five-a-side competitions were in the evenings when the clubs were open. This often resulted in most of the home membership watching the games while hanging from the fencing around the court, baying for the blood of the opposition. Tensions often ran high, and while the Federation often supplied referees for as many games as they could, quite a number of them were not in their prime, and while they were lovely people they often struggled to cope with some of the attitudes of the players who were taking part.

Denis Tuckwell and Derek Pearce were great servants to the Federation. In later years, it was Pete Joslin and Kevin Summerhill – they would turn up and referee regardless of the standard, and at times the Saturday League fixtures could be of a pretty poor quality. Occasionally, and under pressure, Steve would referee – not that he enjoyed it. In fact, I would say that attending football matches with club teams was probably one of his least favourite activities. I remember us playing Hillfields Youth Club on one occasion (we lost again), it was pouring down with rain, the pitch was a mud swamp – and we had nine men. Steve decided to run the line (linesman or assistant referee as they are now called). I think he did it to give us some protection, as the referee, who was probably no more than seventeen years of age, was a bit dubious. He never had a proper linesman's flag so used his handkerchief. It was probably at about 14 – 0, and after being called a dickhead by the young referee on a number of occasions, then finally being told to 'stick his flag up his ass', that he gave up. It didn't quite end there as he was then bitten on the ankle by a dog – oh, and we lost 28 – 0. On another occasion he refereed one of our adults' matches against Brentry Lodge Youth Centre, in the Church of England League, as it was then known. It was between Christmas and New Year and there was snow on the pitch. Now, Steve didn't go a bundle on swearing, and after about fifteen minutes their captain looked up to him and said, "Are you the local fucking vicar?" Steve was not amused, called the two captains together and announced, "One more swear word, and I'm off" – and he meant it.

The other thing that would be lost on most young footballers now is the fact that at Bedminster Down we had to put our own football posts up. The pitch was marked out by the City Council Parks Department, but there were no changing rooms and they didn't put the posts up. The changing rooms weren't a problem as we had changing rooms at the club, some hundred yards away – but the players had to put the posts up themselves. The older teams didn't have much of an issue but the under-12s and under-14s did – as most of them weren't tall enough. It was a great sight to see four of the little 'uns struggle to carry the cross bar down to the pitch, then to cross a main road before descending down to the playing surface. They would then select the biggest, or tallest of them – and then perch somebody on their shoulders to hang the net on the crossbar. Every effort was made to ensure the games went ahead regardless of the weather condition. In the early years, the council would do an inspection on the Friday but that eventually faded out and we undertook our own inspection. Many games went ahead after we had spent hours sweeping snow from the lines. On other occasions after heavy rain, huge puddles would appear in certain parts of the pitch and the seagulls would settle on them. The Brush Brigade would start sweeping the water out of the puddles on to other areas.

There were strict regulations about the changing rooms

– no boots were to be worn inside the club. A large sign was always displayed on match days: 'NO BOOTS TO BE WORN INSIDE THE CLUB'. Anyone ignoring the instruction was suitably reprimanded. A football team gave Steve his first challenge back in 1964, and throughout his time as leader it would be football teams that would continue to test his patience more than any other sport.

3

Sport

Sport is a key element of most organisations wishing to attract young males into its front doors. BDBC probably provided more different sports over the years than most others of a similar size. Equipped with a small gym when it reopened in 1964, it was extended on three occasions to take maximum benefit from its footprint.

An underground rifle range was constructed under the gym floor just after it opened, with the aid of Alf Fripp, a local businessman. The final extension provided a multi-gym facility when it was opened by the comedian/entertainer Gary Wilmot in 1986. Along the way, the gym and the rest of the club was adapted on a regular basis to accommodate a variety of sports.

While football was the main sporting activity arranged by the Bristol Federation of Boys' Clubs (which then became the Avon & Bristol Federation of Boys' Clubs, then the Avon & Bristol Federation of Clubs for Young People and then Young Bristol), most other mainstream sports were organised by them in some way. Steve was a great supporter of the Bristol Federation of Boys' Clubs (BFBC) for many years, a relationship based on the years he spent working there before he became leader at Bedminster Down. The BFBC operated from the old Robinson's offices in Dunn's Buildings, Thomas Lane, Bristol in those days. Chris Wilcox was the then-general secretary, and Roger Summerell, who had replaced John

Wathen in 1971 as assistant secretary, was responsible for organising the activities. Roger also operated a shop within the building for the sale of sports equipment. Roger was a great character. He liked a beer and a fag, and would often swap dirty jokes with club members who would go into the Fed. He was a complete contrast to Chris, who was a Justice of the Peace, and a socialite. Chris also held a position as general secretary for the Gloucestershire Football Association (GFA), before becoming a member of the Football Association (FA). However, no matter how many times I suggested it to Chris; I never once got any FA Cup Final tickets.

We would enter nearly every tournament organised by the Fed. Road-relay and cross-country races, rugby, cricket, swimming, athletics, darts, table tennis, basketball, etc. However, it was a sport not organised by the Fed, that became one of the club's greatest successes – volleyball.

Volleyball was introduced to BDBC by Ray Tingley. Ray was a teacher at Somervale School in Midsomer Norton, before going to Speedwell School in Bristol, where he also ran the very successful Speedwell Volleyball Club. The reason Steve was attracted to the sport of volleyball in the first instance was that he very much thought this sport was accessible to all. You didn't have to be particularly fit, or gifted as a sportsman – you just stood one side of a net, and hit a ball back and forth, and that was how volleyball at BDBC started. Additionally, it didn't even start as a sport on the time-table for the membership – it was played on a Friday night, after the general club had shut at 10pm, and would sometimes go on to the early hours of the morning. Some privileged older members would be allowed to stay behind and join in. In fact, it was at one of these late sessions that many of us were introduced to a certain David Baker, who was later to become the club's chairman. David was involved within youth service in Bristol and visited the club one Friday evening. Being there at the time the club was closing, Steve invited him to watch the volleyball taking place in the gym. The exact details of what happened next are lost in time but the sight of this extremely tall spectacled gentleman wearing a suit and dickey-bow with probably size fifteen feet taking part in his first and probably only volleyball session will not be lost by those who witnessed it.

Like all other sports, if you want to improve you need to compete. There weren't many local volleyball teams at that time. There was obviously Speedwell School (which became Speedwell Volleyball Club), a team from Whitfield, the Church of Latter Day Saints (Whitchurch) had a team, and there was a team at Wootton Bassett. The club's gym wasn't really big enough for the sport, which became a huge advantage for home games, but we made the best use of it.

Through the natural enthusiasm of the early players, a particular love of the game by a few individuals, volleyball took off big-time.

Gerry Greer was one of the younger club helpers. Known as Esky by everyone, Gerry lived locally and joined the club as a member when it first opened. Being one of the younger helpers many of us had a great affinity with him. He hadn't had an easy childhood and had been brought up by his grandparents, just a few doors from the back entrance to Bedminster Down School. He loved the club – and the club loved him. He was very practical, serving an engineering apprenticeship at Bristol Tool & Gauge as a toolmaker. He could repair cars, and loved sport. To cap his talents, he could play a few chords on a guitar and would do a rendition of The Animals' – *House of the Rising Sun*.

Now, Gerry loved volleyball (he also loved canoeing, football, and plenty of other sports as well) but volleyball became a passion, and as his passion grew so did the ability of those around him. Steve, despite his disability, would join in every Friday night – our leader was hooked on the sport. What it did need was an organised league in Bristol, and there wasn't one. So, in 1969, with Steve Long as its first secretary, the Bristol Volleyball League was launched – the brainwave of our local Bedminster Down Boys' Club . It had eleven teams in its first year, with the club having two teams, A and B. We were also founder members of the South West Amateur Volleyball Association in February 1969.

At the end of its first season in April 1970, the first Bristol volleyball tournament took place and was a tremendous success. Our volleyball team continued to build on its success, and became our National Federation's National Champions on more than one occasion. Bob Smith, who started playing as a fourteen-year-old member, went on to play for the National Volleyball Team, while my old mate Barry, became a qualified coach and still plays the game some forty years later.

Unfortunately, with success comes problems – especially when it's sporting success at BDBC. A mixture of helpers and members playing in a local league and playing their home games at the club wasn't a problem. However, as I said earlier, the club's gym wasn't really big enough and if the team and the players were to develop, they would need a bigger gym. This would mean playing their home games away from the club. Steve would not accept this; once again he had reached an impasse with sporting success. The volleyball team left and played their home games at Whitchurch Sports Centre.

While enjoying relative sporting success in the Annual Inter-Club Tournaments, sporting success outside of this eluded me for much of my time as a member. There were a couple of exceptions.

In May 1971, having won the Bristol and then the South West Football five-a-side tournament, we travelled to Nottingham to represent the South West at the National Finals. The bugbear was it was Cup Final day, Arsenal v Liverpool (who organised that date?). We didn't reach the final – we came third. My memory of that day was that we played Scotland in the semi-final. We went 1 – 0 down early on and they then decided they weren't going to let us have the ball. They were awesome and went on to win it. I played in goal and the others were Phil 'Dapper' Davies, Jeff Trought, Tony Cole and, I think, Mervyn Cook. Andy Seer was our manager and he gave up his day to travel with us on the train to Nottingham.

My other success was something that still fills me with pride. It was 1967 and I was fourteen years old. The Fed was having their rugby sevens competition, two age groups – under-15s and under-19s. The problem was that we didn't have enough players for either age group. Frank Evans was a club helper who had joined the staff to do weightlifting. The club had a set of weights and, under Frank's watchful eye, the older members were allowed to use them. Frank loved rugby and was keen for the club to enter a team in the competition. So, he dragged along a colleague from work that had played a bit of rugby, as coach, Graham Meece. I think that Steve was a bit embarrassed that Frank had gone through all this effort and we never had enough players for a team in either age group. "Why don't you join forces?" he suggested. To be honest, I don't think I gave it a lot of thought. Looking back, it was madness. Three fourteen-year-olds, one seventeen-year-old, and three eighteen-year-olds making up an under-19s team! The rest is permanently written in the club's history.

There were only four teams in the under-19s category. We defeated Ashley Down in the semi-final and had to play Brentry Lodge Youth Centre in the final. The date for the final was 28 April 1967 at the Bristol Memorial Ground, home of Bristol Rugby. It was the same night as the Bristol Combination seven-a-side competition.

What we didn't know was that this Bristol Combination event would attract several thousand spectators, and that our opponents pulled most of their players from Aretians Rugby Club.

On the night, we had two other problems. Firstly, the club

didn't have any rugby shirts, so we ran out on to the pitch in front of a few thousand spectators attired in bright tangerine football shirts. Secondly, which seems incredible now looking back, we didn't have a bloody rugby ball. So while our opponents warmed up by running up and down throwing rugby balls and stretching their obvious steroid enhanced muscles, we stood in the middle of the pitch listening to the abuse being aimed at us from the terraces. (That's when I realised they sell beer at rugby grounds.) Of course, we were also well supported by rosette-wearing mums, canteen ladies and a few hardy members. Regrettably, I don't think any of our female supporters had been to a rugby match before – my mother wasn't the only one of them who spent the whole match looking for the goalkeeper and wondering what was actually going on!

Under 19's seven-a-side rugby team in 1967

We kicked off, they caught the ball, and with what seemed five passes, some hairy-arsed player was putting the ball down between our posts. It couldn't have started any worse – the heckling seemed to reach an astonishing level. We kicked off again, and it wasn't long before their six foot winger was haring down the wing seemingly destined to score in the corner. What happened then will stick in my mind for the rest of my life. Geoff Chappell was the under-17s football team's goalkeeper, and he was brave. Out of the corner of my eye, I saw Geoff racing across the pitch, and from what seemed an incredible distance away, he dived through mid-air completely horizontally. He hit this winger in the midriff sending him crashing over the touchline and out of play just a yard from the try line. At that point, the whole crowd erupted, and turned completely on our side. We won by eighteen points to sixteen and I cried. I still recall that night with absolute pride – the squad was Steve Coles, Gerry Greer, Mike 'Joe' Thompson, Geoff Chappell, Brian 'Kraut' Williams, Mike Tomlin, and myself.

Clubs like Bedminster Down provided a unique opportunity for their members to enjoy a variety of sports that wouldn't normally be available to them. Mainstream schools only normally offered rugby, football and cricket – a sport for every term. At Bedminster Down School we benefited from a swimming pool – the size of a postage stamp, but a pool at least. If it rained and you couldn't get on the school field we had the pleasure of doing country dancing! While in 2014 the thought of dancing with some sweet lass in your year group may well stir the nether loins – back in my days, it was the last thing you would want to be doing. Girls had their playground; we had ours – never the two to meet.

When it opened its doors in 1964, one of the most popular sports was caving, or pot-holing (I suppose there is a difference). In fact, it was that popular it had its own identity and badge – The Down Under Club. The club was introduced to the activity by Tony and Anne Oldham. Equipped with carbide lamps, the groups used to venture down Swildon's,

Goatchurch and Rod's Pot on numerous outings. These more off the wall activities were a huge attraction to some members, especially those who didn't play the normal field sports. Don Rogers was an early helper and became a keen caver. Don and Stella lived opposite the club in Brunel Road. Dave, their son, was a member when the club opened. Not to be outdone, their daughter, Margaret, joined her mum as a member of the ladies group, and she dragged her husband Roy along to help. This early community support was to become the backbone of the club through the rest of its existence. From a personal point of view, I can't say that I was ever a keen participant in pot-holing. In fact, it was not until around 1982 that I ventured underground and that was only because I had taken a group of juniors to the club's cottage for the weekend and thought I ought to lead by example. It was at that weekend that I also had a go at abseiling – just the once, I hasten to add!

Caving and pot-holing, abseiling and canoeing became an everyday part of club life. The club always managed to find

Club members on a canoeing trip at Tal-y-sarn

a suitable enthusiastic adult to keep the momentum going for most activities. In the case of caving and abseiling, it was Tony Fouracres and Barry Lovell. There was inevitably a driving force behind most of the activities, just like there was in volleyball. And as far as canoeing was concerned, it was again Gerry Greer who led the way. At one point, the craft room was turned into the canoe-making room! Moulds were purchased and before long, members were building their own canoes. You could always tell when they were building canoes due to the smell of the solvents they were using. Health and Safety precautions weren't that stringent and I'm sure some of them who were involved used to appear from the craft room with rolling eyes and vague expressions as a consequence of being in there too long. I managed to get into a canoe twice. It was on the same trip to Saltford, near Bath. The River Avon was like a mill pond – and I fell in twice within about two minutes of setting off – never again.

When I think of the concerns there are nowadays regarding the fitness of our young people, it's difficult not to be cynical about the opportunities that clubs like ours provided over the years, and the purists decided that they were no longer needed. We did it all, not always successfully – but we had a go.

We had cricket equipment and used to participate in the Fed's six-a-side competition. Roy James played for Bedminster Cricket Club for many years and one summer he asked us if we would take a team down to The Clanage (the home of Bedminster Cricket Club) to play their youth team. I was around fifteen at the time. When we got to the ground, the contrasts were immense – there were the Bedminster lads impeccably dressed in whites – and we were in jeans and T-shirts. I was on the large side at the time (weight control has never been my strong point). We batted first and Gerry and I got a few, we were especially severe on their two opening bowlers, Tommy Mullread and Andy Pillinger. When it came to our turn to bowl, we had them in a spot of bother. However, their captain was Keith Fear, then a young professional footballer with Bristol City. Keith was never one to keep his opinions to himself and made it clear he was going to get this match over quickly. He did get a few runs but then managed to hit one skywards towards the boundary. I still can't explain how I managed to catch it. I sort of ran around the boundary and fell over with one hand outstretched – and the ball stuck in my hand. Keith departed to the boundary calling me a range of names, most of which included the word fat. The match was watched by Roy James and the wonderful John Budd, who was chairman of Bedminster CC. I started playing for Bedminster a couple of weeks later and Keith and I became great friends – largely because I refused to join his post-match card school!

Cricket was also the choice of game for the staff to play against the members as the club drew to a close for its summer break. At that time, May & Hassel was an annexe to Bedminster Down Secondary School, and serviced by a small white pavilion. In the years that followed, the games moved to the school site itself. The games were always played in great humour (although things could get a bit touchy at times) and for years we benefited in having our own scorer. Daphne Evans served the club as a helper and a member of the management committee for years. She loved cricket and would always come along to do the scoring. Some of the members relished the opportunity to hurl the ball down at great speed against members of staff and some would not take being belted all over the boundary Bothamesque very well. We did have some laughs – on one famous occasion the game was halted because the box the particular helper was wearing to protect his wedding tackle had somehow come adrift, and slipped down the inside of his trousers to be delivered at the crease just as the ball was being delivered. The comments that followed regarding the perceived size of the protector against the size of what it was protecting aren't repeatable! Our cricket equipment wasn't particularly good and I am sure we had the same pads and gloves for about twenty years. The bats were used for the indoor version of the game, played in the gym during the summer, and often had bits missing off the end. The victors would marvel in their accomplishment for the rest of the night, the losers would inspect the score-book to ensure they had not been diddled.

Later, as the years progressed and the interests of members changed, so did some of the activities. We had motocross bikes, BMX Bikes, we went skateboarding and we even had a skateboarding ramp inside the building – the club always adapted its activities to meet the demands of its membership as best it could.

4

Trophies, Tributes and Miffer

I don't actually think I had seen a snooker table until I joined the club, (Pot Black wasn't televised until 1969) and while they weren't what you could classify as full-size, they were probably 6 foot by 3 foot in old money. The three the club had during the early days formed the bedrock of activities that took place inside the heart of the building most nights – the main club area. There wasn't room to have the table tennis tables out permanently, so that activity took place in the gym one night a week, normally a Friday.

The main canteen area was the hub of everything that went on in the club throughout its time. A visit to the area would give you a sense of the mood of the members instantly and in the early years the atmosphere was electric. Three snooker tables, a dart board, table football, members playing draughts, chess and other board games. The music came from our single-decked record player, the disc jockey for many a year being the one and only Phil 'Miffer' Smith. Unfortunately the record player was housed near the business end area, the canteen. There was a constant battle between the canteen ladies and Miffer over the volume control. Miffer, our Downs Syndrome member, is a part of the club's rich history. Oddly enough we shared the same birth date although he was a year older than me. Steve's story of Miffer in 'Miff the Biff', gives a unique insight to the whole story of Philip (to give him his real name) Smith's life at BDBC, and even all these years on is still a wonderful read.

Philip lived just around the corner from the club in Felton Grove. His parents approached Steve when the club opened to enquire about him joining as a member – the rest, as they say, is history. He remained part of all our lives at the club until 1978 – he could be exasperating, he could be a pain in the ass – but everyone loved him. He came on Whitsun Camps with us, even to Cornwall on a number of occasions. When Philip's mother died, he moved into a home in Newlands Road, Withywood, not far from Steve's home. He eventually moved from there to another residence in Lockleaze and it was there that I tracked him down in May 1989 to attend Steve's retirement dinner. I hadn't seen Philip for a number of years, (since 1982 when I arranged for him to attend the club's reunion dinner). When he moved from Withywood, the so-called experts discouraged contact. Years later, I can understand their point of view to a degree. Philip needed to build an independent life. However, I wanted, if I could, to get him to Steve's retirement night and so I tracked down where he was living and with the help of his social worker met him over a number of weekends at his home. We arranged for a taxi to collect Philip and his guest from his home and return them after. And so, some eleven years after he had left, he returned to BDBC for only the second time – and of course, he upstaged everyone!

It was Miffer who delivered one of the greatest put-me-downs that I have ever had – and I think the tale is still worth repeating all these years on. Only recently I had the pleasure of playing Father Christmas at Cheddar Grove School. The startled look on some of the young faces as I casually wandered through the school's corridors was amazing. Anyway, around the same time as I was strutting my stuff as Father Christmas for Diane Scarborough's playgroup at Backwell – so was the same lady running the then-current ladies group at the club. I was therefore tasked with performing the role of the great man at the club's Christmas Fayre. The club's quiet room was turned into Santa's grotto and the children would line up to

The one and only Philip 'Miffer' Smith

see Father Christmas – for a fee. This particular year, Philip joined the queue. Being tipped off in advance by Steve, I made sure that my outfit was adjusted and prepared for his entrance. I thought it all went very well, lots of ho-ho, a deep Santa voice, and very little eye contact (Miffer could be very astute). I wished my visitor a good Christmas at the end of our brief encounter, off he marched, present in hand. What happened next is best described by Steve:

"It was about two minutes later that Philip came dodging through the crowds down the whole length of the club and into the office. When he was excited he would extend his arms down to their full length and flap his hands out a forty-five degree angle as his whole body stretched with glee. It was like a waddling penguin and the kids always adopted this pose if they wanted to imitate Philip –knees stiff, chest out, hands like two elevation flaps. And the inevitable ear-to-ear grin, just to set it off. This was Philip's state as he burst into my office and blurted out in hushed pants 'Steve, Steve,' (tense pause) 'Steve, Steve,' (look around at the door to see if anyone is hearing), 'Steve, Steve,' (extremely hushed, confidential whisper) 'Father Christmas is Andy Lewis.'"

Steve, being no beginner at amateur dramatics himself, reeled back in shock, before entering in a one way dialogue with Philip, that Father Christmas was in fact Father Christmas and not Andy Lewis, and more to the point was on a very special visit to Bedminster Down Boys' Club. All this had gone on while I was still ho-hoing at another part of the club in complete ignorance – I was told later.

Fast forward twelve months. The same event and the same Father Christmas (Di was very convincing, and it was best not to decline the offer to play the role). Philip lined up in the queue with all the other youngsters. Very aware of the previous year's encounter I was well prepared, there was no way Philip would recognise me. Enter the grotto Philip 'Miffer' Smith. We engaged in normal small talk – have you been a good boy? What would you like for Christmas? All the normal stuff that you do when playing Father Christmas. Philip was responding shyly, everything seemed normal and I was absolutely chuffed that he showed no sign of recognising who was beneath the outfit. I gave him his present, which he tucked under his arm, and he headed for the Grotto's exit. Then he stopped, turned and with the most sarcastic smile delivered the classic punchline: "Give my regards to your mother, Andrew!" That was the last time I played Santa at the club.

Miffer had a great love of music, bringing his collection to the club on most nights to play. Each record would be carefully removed from its sleeve, meticulously cleaned, before being played. Great favourites of his were songs from Eurovision – *Puppet on a String*, the classic Sandie Shaw hit was a club classic, and often involved the whole membership joining in the chorus. *Congratulations* by Cliff Richard (again from Eurovision) had the same impact – it used to drive most of the membership bonkers. If you let on that you had a particular favourite, and Miffer liked you, then that could be awkward as well. He used to wait till you came in to the main canteen area and then quietly slip on your favourite record. Songs that Miffer liked himself would often be played ten times a night, and certain records were known to disappear on occasions – much to our favourite DJ's disgust.

It was Philip's love of his records that got him into trouble with the police on one occasion. Philip had been allowed to travel to school by bus as part of an experiment, this was to enhance his independence. However, he had to change buses at the centre and these were the days when there was a row of around six red telephone boxes in a line on the centre. For some reason, Philip decided to enter one of the phone boxes and to ring Mary Sherman, at Threeways Children's Home. Having finished his call, he left the telephone box, leaving his beloved carrier bag of records inside. Before he got on his bus he realised he had forgotten his records and returned to the telephone boxes, entering the wrong one. Thinking his records had disappeared, and remembering those important words every parent says to their children, 'If you are in trouble – ring the police,' he did just that – he rang 999. What happened next can only be really understood if you knew Miffer.

Operator: "Emergency – what service do you require?"
Miffer: "Police."
Police: "Police emergency, how can I help you?"
Miffer: "I have just seen a bank robbery!"

Three squad cars screamed around the corner from Bridewell Police Station, it was 5pm and rush hour. The whole centre came to a halt. Philip eventually made it home but his records were never found. That was the last time Philip went to school on the bus.

In later years, Miffer was actually employed as one of the club's cleaners with specific responsibility for cleaning the quiet room. Now, the quiet room actually started its time as the Alfred Gardiner Quiet Room, after the club received a legacy of money towards its construction from the old Hotwells Boys' Club which had closed. It originally housed a TV, and was supposed to be a quiet area for members to read and relax. Members of the junior club weren't originally allowed to use this room when this section opened (or the rifle range) – it was hallowed ground. The room's use did not predominantly change – although the number of members using it varied considerably. When The Benny Hill Show was at its peak you couldn't get inside the room as hormonal members crammed inside to get a glimpse of any forbidden flesh. On some occasions it would seem like the rest of the club was empty, and then you would hear the mortal words of 'look at the tits on that', and you would realise where everyone was. Top of the Pops was another favourite, along with any football matches. There were arguments over the channel selection – but this was pre-satellite, so there were only a few to choose from. It was supposed to be kept clean and tidy by whoever used it but these were mostly teenagers! Anyway, Philip had specific duties for cleaning it on a morning – it would often take him all the morning. He would carefully polish every trophy and every shelf, painstakingly – and on other occasions, he could be found fast asleep with his feet up next to the fire! Turning the fire on was absolute sacrilege and would result in a severe reprimand. To avoid detection, Philip decided to turn the fire around on one occasion so it faced the wall – which resulted in him catching the curtains on fire.

The area where the canteen ladies served was at one end, and the back wall was fitted with sturdy wooden shelves which housed the drinks and all the other confectionary was stacked underneath. Compared to what is available nowadays our choice in the early days seems minimal now but that's not how it felt then. There were the classics of Tizer, Dandelion and Burdock and Pepsi. The sweets were classics of our time (which I still miss) – Black Jacks, Fruit Salads, Shrimps, Sherbet Fountains, Spaceships, Spangles. If you had enough money for chocolate then how about a Five Boys, Bar Six, Treets, Caramac, Loot or Mars. The man from Burtons who supplied the crisps also sold penny teacakes and you could get twelve for a shilling – eating them all at the same time was a challenge.

Small blue tables were situated between the snooker tables and the canteen, with plastic chairs providing the seats for those wishing to sit. Before any of the extensions to the building were built, everything focused around the main club area. Many would argue that the expansion of the club, with three separate extensions resulted in a reduction of the atmosphere. I would counter that the heart of the club was always where the most vibrant work went on – and that was always in the main club area. There would be a booking system during the busy periods for some of the more popular activities – especially snooker and table tennis. The club would fill with over a hundred members on a night-time during its heyday. Occasionally the membership would benefit from a free film show. The bright orange plastic chairs we possessed would be put out in rows and we would all sit down and watch a film. Mr Simmonds, as we all knew him, lived in Ilchester Crescent a couple of doors down from Bett and Bill Hall, and he would arrive at the club with his projector and screen with the latest James Bond movie or something similar. We would all arm ourselves with something from the canteen and settle down for the free show. Unfortunately this was before any smoking bans, so on a winter's evening with no windows open it could get quite stuffy. We actually on one occasion watched The War Game, which was a BBC Documentary made in 1965 depicting the effects of nuclear war on Britain. Made in black and white and lasting fifty minutes, the film depicts the prelude to and the immediate weeks after the aftermath to a Soviet nuclear attack on Britain. The film had been banned in August 1965, and this was probably 1967. It remained un-shown in full on British Television until 1985. The club was packed that Friday night and you could hear a pin drop throughout the showing.

Before the installation of a gas central heating system, the club was heated with electric convector heaters and then later, Calor gas heaters. The building was everything you wouldn't want to have in a modern construction. The original windows were eventually replaced with single glazed aluminium replace-ments – even though in the height of winter the combined effect of 100 kids inside and sub-zero temperature outside along with gas and electric heaters would result in water running down the inside of the windows, the concrete inside walls would run with water too. A further problem was the building's flat roof (replaced as a whole twice and forever being repaired) leaked and we would sometimes find containers dotted around the club – positioned to catch the rain water as it came through the ceiling. Nobody minded – it may not have conformed to current health and safety requirements but this was very much our place.

Surprisingly enough, even when it was jammed to the rafters, there was very little agro. If there were going to be any problems they would normally emanate from the gym – and if it was going to be any activity it would normally be football. Teenagers take on a different mindset when they enter the gym to play football. If we weren't kicking the shit out of one another it would be the poor member of staff who would be getting the bruises. If you were going to take a football session as a member of staff it was safer to stay on the sidelines and blow a whistle. Personal vendettas could be settled – forget fifty yards and pistols, this was twenty -five yards and a football. I remember Nicky Johns and Mark Spear kicking the hell out of each other on more than one occasion and from my era Phil 'Dapper' Davies was known for the odd temperamental outburst. I remember being asked to take an under-16s football session one night, following a problem with the sessions over previous weeks. I was brutal with the fitness bit for the first fifteen minutes or so, thinking it would tire them out a bit – it didn't.

It wasn't only the members that could get lairy in the gym. At one stage the helpers would go in to the gym after the club closed on a Friday night, often staying in when volleyball was at its height when that was the sport of the old 'uns, prior to that it was three-a-side football. Steve always fancied himself a bit of a goalie. Our club leader had always worn glasses and these would often be worn with a piece of Elastoplast holding the arm on to the frame. Steve was often breaking his spectacles. Following weeks of ribbing during this period, Steve decided to splash out on some new specs. On this particular night, Steve entered the gym at the end of club adorned with his new specs – and true to form made a huge song and dance about it. What happened next, I will remember until the end of my days. Steve was at one end in goal for one team and I was at the other. My memory fails me on who the rest of the players were apart from one – Gerry Greer. When Steve was in goal he always had the same stance, feet about eighteen inches apart and arms pointing at about forty-five degrees to his body. Gerry found himself in the middle of the gym, not facing Steve. Suddenly the ball was in the air at perfect volleying height for him and swivelling on one leg like a ballerina he caught the ball perfectly – the trouble was Steve had advanced out of his goal and the ball caught him straight in the middle of his face, sending his brand-new, day-old new specs into several bits all across the gym floor. What followed was an awkward silence and Steve, unamused, storming out.

It wasn't always football that caused problems. I spent five days in hospital on one occasion after being asked to referee a badminton match! It was a Sunday morning and Inter-Club Tournament time. I was asked to referee a couple of senior badminton games. All was fine until there was a gap between games and I was warming up with one of the members (Kevin Hickery) who was waiting for his opponent. Into the gym comes Paul 'Hawkman' Hawker. "I'll warm up with you, Lou," he said. Paul wasn't the most gracious of sportsmen and everything he did came with a Government Health Warning. Before I could deter him, he picked up a badminton racket and was running around the court like a demented fly swatter. Unfortunately, my head was in the way and he brought the racket down straight into my face, well actually my right eye. My eyelid split right across and dropped down and I ended up on the floor. It was my old mate Barry who took me off to the Bristol Royal Infirmary, where I discovered that the impact had caused a blood clot at the back of my eye and I spent the next five days flat on my back in hospital. To make things worse, as there was no way they were going to slide a bed-pan under my ass, I managed to hold on for the next five days, only to find that when they eventually let me out of bed that I was severely bunged up. I then had to suffer the indignity of having a female nurse stick a plastic tube up my ass to 'assist with the natural process'. Bloody Hawkman!

When the club was originally constructed, you could only view the activities in the gym from the club lobby, through two small windows in a pair of doors. Years later, when the first extension was built, long viewing panels were put in the gym's side and rear walls making all the activities more visible and improving the connectivity between all the areas.

The Inter-Club Tournaments were always popular – there would be individual competitions, doubles and some team games. You couldn't enter as a team, names were drawn from a hat for the teams and doubles events. Competitions covered the full range of gym activities and board games, including draughts, chess and eventually noodling. The origins of noodling were simply as a result of waiting lists. During the periods when you were waiting to use the snooker tables, table tennis tables etc, we would sit and yack at one of the many small tables in the canteen. Out of boredom one night, someone started bouncing a table tennis ball into a glass from the canteen. A game then ensued with a member either side of the table seeing who could bounce the table tennis ball into the glass the most times – and noodling had been discovered. One minute either way for the rounds and two minutes for the final.

Inter-Club Tournaments' trophies were presented at the club's Open Night. In the early years, this was at a formal dinner, with a meal being prepared and served by the ladies' group. Tables were laid out in the club's gym and members would join the club's voluntary staff and invited guests at a sit-down dinner. As members, we were expected to be smartly dressed and photographs show many of us with shirts and ties at fourteen years of age. At the end of the proceedings, the ladies would often be served their meal by the male members of staff. The trophies were small black plaques with a medal in the middle depicting the sport and the winner's name would be engraved below. They were well sought-after and I'm sure there will be hundreds lingering in the bottoms of wardrobes even now.

Over the years that followed, there was an increase in the number of donated or memorial trophies being awarded. One of the first I can remember was the Five Brothers' Cup – Wesley, Jeffrey, Terry, Martin and Stephen Windows were five brothers who were club members. At the time, this was a first for the club and the family presented a trophy to be awarded at the club's annual dinner. If my memory serves me right, I think it was awarded for fundraising but, either way, it was the first of many. Tragically many of the trophies that followed were in memory of members of the club family that had died. On open nights that followed, representatives of the deceased family would come and present their trophies. Often those members attending had little or indeed no knowledge of those that had passed but they always treated the occasion with the utmost respect.

Dealing with bereavement within the club was never easy and it was something I know that Steve found difficult. The first memorial had been the one to Colin, Shirley and Andrew Jones. They were among the 108 victims of the Swiss Air Disaster on the 10 April 1973. Colin was a helper and a vibrant, energetic member of the club's management committee. Shirley was a member of the ladies' group and Andrew a junior club member. I had never been to a funeral before. I remember walking with others from the club along Brunel Road to the Zion Methodist Church on Bishopsworth Road, a place that I was very familiar with. Along with others from the club's community, we paid our respects to those we had lost. It was the first of many times I would do this over the years that followed. A plaque was erected before the building of the new changing rooms and garage, opened in their honour. Many years later, Steve confided that he was concerned that the club shouldn't become a mausoleum, with the walls covered with memorial plaques, and he certainly didn't want anything with his name on it should anything ever happen to him. However, the reality was that the members always found an appropriate way of remembering those that had passed, when that was appropriate. And, regardless of what he thought, there was never going to be any chance that the club that Steve had built would not find a way of recognising that work when he passed away – and they did.

When the club eventually closed we tried to give as many of the trophies as possible back to those families at the Final Dinner.

5

Threeways, Highwinds and Cuffley

Chris Sherman got involved in the club through Dave Phillips, who was a social worker. Chris had a sister, Mary, and she was the housemother at a children's home in Broomhill – Threeways.

As a result of this, the club built a relationship – a wonderful relationship with Threeways, and also with the Highwinds Children's Home in Highridge, run by Helen Ball. Members were fully exposed to the lives of children that were far different from their own. We would take the children to Weston, the zoo and invite them to shows at the club. Some senior members became regular visitors to the Threeways home in Broomhill. If you went by bus, it was two bus journeys – from Bedminster Down to Temple Meads and then another bus from outside the railway station to Broomhill. Sunday afternoons was always a favourite time to visit but the buses could be a bit iffy.

It was a visit to Threeways that gave me my first experience of being a pillion passenger on the back of a motorbike. I was just about to leave the club one sunny Sunday afternoon to wander down Cheddar Grove to get the bus to Temple Meads when Esky announced that he was going to Threeways and did I want a lift? Now, Esky had a motorbike and when I said, "That would be great" (saving me the bus fare), he quickly added – "You have been on the back of a bike before, Lou?" I nodded quickly and stuck his spare helmet on my head, as his comments about keeping the bike balanced faded behind my safety headwear. The rules of balance seemed simple to me – if you put weight on one side – you balance things by putting the same weight on the opposite side. So off we set, some straight bits of road and some not so straight. When we went around a right-hand bend and Esky banked the bike to the right, I confidently leaned the opposite way! As you can imagine we didn't make the whole journey to Broomhill without Esky having to pull over, near Temple Meads, I think. The conversation then went something along the lines of, "What the ********* hell are you doing?" When I tried to explain that I was simply applying some law of physics he seemed unimpressed. I then received my first lesson on what I was required to do to ensure we both arrived at our destination in one piece. I don't think I was ever offered a lift on the back of his bike again – can't think why!

It took me years to understand the true plight of some of the children at Threeways, and later those at New Park House in Hertfordshire. I was probably fourteen when I paid my first visit to Threeways. Some of the kids were virtually the same age as me and I struggled to understand why they were there. Mary was a great character, she had a great sense of humour but it must have been hard work. It was the winter of 1968 when I paid a visit to another children's home, this time in London.

Jack Yandell was a former leader of Manor Farm Boys' Club and he and his wife, Kaye, were friends of Steve. They were houseparents at a children's home in London, or actually Cuffley, in Hertfordshire. It was called New Park House. If I remember correctly, Jack had visited the club with a few of the children at some point. Steve announced that he was going to visit Jack and Kaye at Cuffley and asked myself and Martin 'Leggy' Hill if we wanted to join him. Martin Hill was a year older than me and a mate. He was brought up with his family in Willada Close, Bedminster but had moved to Withywood when his parents' marriage broke down. His grandparents lived just along the road from the club in Brunel Road. Martin was tall, very tall – hence the nickname Leggy.

He was one of the most genuine and the kindest of lads I ever met in my time at BDBC.

These were the days before motorways, so we travelled the journey to Cuffley up the A4. Steve had a Morris Minor van, adapted for his disability. I spent the whole journey in the back, which had no seats – and I bloody froze. New Park House was a beautiful building in the leafy suburb of Cuffley. It catered for around sixteen children of both sexes, from around six to sixteen, and mostly from extremely deprived multi-racial backgrounds in Islington. Being Christmas time, the house was decorated throughout – loads of Christmas trimmings and a huge Christmas tree in the lounge. The home was on three levels, with the upper level being the private quarters of Jack and Kaye. Across the first landing there was a huge net – full of coloured balloons.

"I love the decorations," I commented to Jack, or Fred as everyone called him, "especially the net full of balloons." The reply will haunt me for years to come. "That net is not for the balloons, Andy, it's to catch the kids when they throw themselves off the top floor." Listening to Fred talk about the kinds of backgrounds of the children there – violence, prostitution, incest and drug-taking, was difficult. That first night in New Park House I spent hours listening to the screams of a young boy called Tony (not his real name). He would sit on the floor pulling pieces of flesh out of his chest.

New Park House certainly held a different group of children than Threeways. Jack and Harry (not their real names) were eleven when they held up a jeweller in London with a sawn-off shotgun. There were a number of family groups, brother and sister, brothers etc. I had got to know Mike (again, not his real name) when he had visited the club. As members, you could get roped in to providing entertainment for visitors, organising games and just providing an ear for them to talk to – that's how I learned the story behind Jack and Harry. In Mike's case, his mother had died and his dad couldn't cope, so he and his younger brother found themselves at New Park House. Mike was eleven years old. I continued to keep in contact with him for as long as I could. Leggy was equally moved by his visit to Cuffley. Later that year, he joined the Royal Marines and supported New Park House for years afterwards.

Certainly there appeared to be big differences between the issues that faced the youngsters in Cuffley to those in Bristol. At fifteen years of age, I certainly wasn't in any position to understand the complex issues that these youngsters were facing at that time, or how it would impact on the rest of their lives. Talking to Jack and Kaye years later, they presented me with an image certainly of Mike that I didn't recognise. I wasn't in a position to contradict them; they knew him much better than I did. I still wonder now what happened to him and his younger brother.

I learned a lot from my visits to Highwinds and New Park House.

6

Voluntary Staff

The club pulled most of its voluntary staff from the local community. My dad was an early helper, running a woodwork class one night a week, and there were quite a few father/son, helper/member combinations within the club early on. There were Bett and Bill Hall and their son, Brian. Charlie and Winnie Coles and their son, Steve. Ray and June Sandy and their son, Martin. Maurice and Audrey Thompson and their son, Mike. Olive Sollars helped behind the canteen and she had two sons at the club, Mike and Pete. Ada Hurditch ran the early ladies' group and her son, Bert, was a member. It was a common phenomenon that went on for many years. Whether it was good for the members involved, I'm not so sure. For me, it did cause a problem but more about that later. The voluntary staff can pride themselves that they were the cornerstone of the club's success over the coming years. Early on, it would be parents who provided that vital support. However, Steve was keen to develop the potential of his older senior members. Most of the older members that joined in 1964 were part of the senior football team and they quickly moved on to other things. While parents (especially mums in the canteen) provided a vital resource for specific activities, running football teams, caving, etc, Steve needed the engagement of the older members as his conduit to the current membership. And he was blessed with an abundance of quality early on.

They were a diverse group, Sherman, Esky, Waffler, Pippo, Our Rog, Andy Seer – at times it was like a madhouse.

Looking back over forty years later, it was easy to see why they were so successful. First, and hugely important, they were all single. Secondly, they all gave their time freely, without question. And lastly, for all of them in their own unique ways, they could all engage with the membership.

I have sometimes been asked, 'Why do you do it, why do you give your time, how do you find the time, what does your wife think?' Whilst discussing the concept of doing voluntary work. Some of those questions are easy to answer – I enjoyed it. You can get all wrapped up in the great statements about giving back to the community and that entire moral claptrap – but I actually believe most people do it because they enjoy it. And when they stop enjoying it, they stop doing it. There were times for me when the enjoyment wasn't as good as other times. I would take a break, step back – still support, but from a distance. Unfortunately some staff found it hard to do that, to ease off, take a break – and withdrew permanently. Obviously, with an ever-moving membership, volunteers that were parents would disappear, but not always. I was lucky to have worked with a huge variety of voluntary staff over the years. I have particular reasons to thank two of them.

There were a few paid assistant leaders at the club. Two of them, in particular, were outstanding workers with young people but they were different in many ways. Gerry Greer was the first paid assistant leader at BDBC.

The club was brimming, there was nearly always a waiting list, and financial support had been awarded for an assistant for Steve. An advert was placed and applicants encouraged. Gerry had been a stalwart among the voluntary staff but still working as a toolmaker at Bristol Tool & Gauge. He was an obvious candidate for the role and there was unanimous support for his appointment.

Even now, I'm not sure whether he understands the impact

he had on some of the members when he was there. There were, of course, those that hero worshipped him, they were mostly the volleyball purists and the canoeists. Gerry hadn't had it easy as a youngster and I'm sure he would say that the club provided a vital outlet for him as a member, when things could have gone astray. He was able to fill that gap between the members and the leader with consummate ease. He was a great sportsman, he had a sense of humour, he would throw himself into what was required and, importantly for me, he was loyal, trustworthy and a natural leader of young people.

However, for Gerry there were two major problems. Firstly he wasn't qualified, as far as the Local Education Authority was concerned, and secondly, because of the first, 'the pay was shit.' To supplement his pay, Gerry used to repair cars. My first car was an Austin A40, which benefited a couple of times from his skilled hands.

Gerry stayed in the post for less than a year, before returning to a role in engineering. The club had been successful to date with producing its voluntary staff from within, and although there could be an argument looking back that Gerry's appointment was more about sentiment than logic (how did anyone think he was going to survive on the money and have a life outside of the club at the same time?), the appointment of somebody from outside the club's community seemed absolutely bizarre at the time. Of course, the idea that somebody who was a paid worker would want a life outside of the club was lost on our club leader. He devoted his entire life – day and night – to the club, and while the appointment of an assistant would give him a day and night off, it was only 'off', in that it was away from the club.

Steve found it difficult to accept that some of his newly appointed staff had a life outside of the club, which involved the opposite sex. For much of the early years, the young voluntary staff had dedicated their entire life outside of work to supporting the club and its leader. They had been there in the evenings, weekends, they had supported outside activities and club trips and holidays.

The natural progression from senior member to voluntary helper was at the age of twenty-one. For those members that were still going to the club at that age, it was obvious they were giving more than they were getting – so becoming a voluntary member of staff was a natural landmark – if, of course, you fitted the club leader's criteria.

While the likes of Dave Phillips, Chris Sherman, Andy Seer and Roger Grimley were already in the staff team when I joined, others like Esky, Scarby (Dave Scarborough,) Phil 'Pippo' Stacey and Paul Allen all made the transition during my early membership. The change of role was marked by the presentation of an NABC tie by Steve to his new cohorts.

My progression to a member of the voluntary staff team was less auspicious. I had a fractious relationship with Steve while I was a member. Being the son of an existing helper was not always helpful – being referred to as so-and-so's son, or as in my case 'Little Lou', could be wearing. In fact he really did piss me off. I suppose as a teenager I could have been described as bolshie, loud, arrogant, self-opinionated – and even worse. I have had strong feelings about the right of everyone to have their own identity all my life – it's not right that young people are judged against their parents. I accepted that my father was a voluntary helper and a member of the club's management committee – so what!? Looking back many, many years it's obvious that I did piss Steve off at times, and it was often Gerry, and then Brian Howarth's wise counsel that managed to balance the equilibrium. I find it ironic now that Steve's passion for ensuring the members had their say, which transcribed later in to the club's revolutionary parliament, always had to be balanced against his ultimate right to manage the club. My old mate Barry Lovell had joined the club after me, another teenager from the 266th Zion Methodist Scouts who decided to hang up his woggle and try new ventures. Now,

I will be the first to accept that Barry has some natural abilities that I don't have – now an accomplished canoeist, volleyball coach, skier, etc (although he was shit at football). But was it right that he was appointed a member of voluntary staff before me? I didn't think so at the time. I was attending the club five nights a week; two of the nights were to help Dave Phillips run the junior club. Barry still maintains he never got his tie – I know I didn't (and Scarby tells me he didn't get one either).

I became a voluntary member of staff as a consequence of Dave Phillips leaving. Dave assembled the junior leader team to discuss the situation and who could take over – all assembled suggested I should do it, so I did. Steve was not amused, I could tell, but he reluctantly accepted the decision and probably against his better judgement, I became a member of the voluntary staff team (without an NABC tie) at nineteen – but the clashes between Steve and me would not end there.

Gerry's replacement was Brian Howarth, a Londoner. Brian wasn't going to be the only appointment of someone from outside the club community into the post of assistant leader over the years – but his was the only appointment that really worked. In short, Brian was a class act as a youth worker.

At the outset, many thought that the odds against Brian being successful would be limited. He didn't come from the community; he didn't even live in Bristol. There was an argument that he didn't speak our language – after all he had a strong London accent. Probably what many of us didn't understand at that time was the reputation that this rather small single sexed club on a South Bristol housing estate was getting, along with its leader. Brian came to Bedminster Down because of that reputation – it was a match made in heaven.

Brian was dynamic and a natural leader of young people. He was a great confidante, somebody that would not judge you but would give an honest, balanced opinion if asked. I ran the junior section my way. I have already told you

I was bolshie back then. Steve did not always agree with some of the decisions I would make. I remember popping into the club one dinner hour; both Steve and Brian were there. "Can I have a word?" Steve said ushering me into the quiet room at the front of the building. I have no idea what was said but remember him telling me that he was the club leader and I would run the juniors his way. Let's just say that voices were raised and words exchanged. I stormed out slamming the front doors of the club – they were glass and I remember the whole front of the building seeming to shake as I walked across the car park.

I can't remember if it was a few hours later or the next day that I telephoned the club and Brian answered. We talked and talked. He gave me his advice and I followed it. Steve and I made our peace and I never rowed with him again. (I didn't say that I never ever disagreed with him again, just never rowed.) Brian worked with me at junior club and joined me on a couple of junior club holidays. His time spent at Winford Grove was too short – he moved on to be a successful leader in his own right. When Steve retired in 1989, Brian was the only person I, and others who knew him, wanted for the job – but he wasn't going to be persuaded and, again, his decision was probably the right one.

There were other paid assistants after Brian and without being in anyway disrespectful to any of them, they never matched the natural ability of the first two – and years later the club ended the position.

The voluntary helpers who worked at the club during its existence at Winford Grove, right up until the final days, should never underestimate the role they played in its success. If I had my way I would put a permanent memorial at what was the club site, publicly thanking the community of Bedminster Down and those who served its club in a voluntary basis over the years.

On reflection, it would be easy to split the role of adults

within the club into two time periods: 1964 – 1989 and 1990 – 2004, mirroring the two full-time leaders the club had over that period. More about the leaders later but what about the voluntary staff?

The early, older helpers there when the club opened in 1964, mostly parents, were eventually replaced by the first breed of young helpers from within the club. Some of those early helpers continued to support the club for years after, others naturally left as their sons moved on. Alan Meacham was a parent who got involved with the club through his son, Rob. Alan helped me run the junior section for a period and his wife, Marion, served the club for many years as the cleaner. There were many parents that served the club over the years. Ernie Hensleigh had two sons as members, Mark and Ian. Ernie helped for many years, even running a football team. To make sure she wasn't left at home, his wife, Pauline, joined the ladies' group. Ernie would fall into the general good egg category alongside the likes of John Hemmings (who was a chef – which benefited our Cornwall Holidaymakers one year), Eddie Burton, Alan Jefferies and the evergreen Tom Merchant, who helped out in the junior club for many a year.

The ladies' group would continue to change over the club's life, evolving around the ladies helping at that time. They would organise jumble sales and bazaars in aid of club funds – they were a huge financial support to the club over the years.

Jumble sales would be a scream in the early days. The ladies would take possession of the club on a Friday night and they would all assemble to sort the collected jumble. It would be laid out on trestle tables, all marked up at the selling price. The better garments, I'm sure, were filtered off for private sale. On the Saturday afternoon, responding to local ads, a huge queue would assemble at the club's front door – waiting to pay 6d (that's 2.5p in new money) to get in. Anyone playing football for the club teams at home on that day used to have to dodge a large group of people, assembled like a rugby scrum at the front door. There were regular faces and people you would recognise from your own community. June and Bill (my neighbours at home) were regular attendees – I often think they expected to be made aware of any hidden bargains before the doors opened. The other strange thing is that although all the items were obviously second-hand and cheap, some people couldn't help wanting to nick them. As a consequence, Steve and Stella Rogers (who ran the ladies' group) would spend the afternoon marching up and down the aisles looking for shoplifters. There were the regular dodgy customers and a few that were banned from coming again for nicking stuff. At the end of the sale, everything was divided into two piles – a pile to be kept for the next sale and a pile to go to the scrap rag man in Feeder Road.

The Ladies Group 1965

The ladies group would cook all the food and serve meals at the early annual dinners, help dress the cast at shows and run fundraising events. However, clashes with the full-time leader were not uncommon. In later years, some of the ladies got a bit above their station for Steve and feathers were plucked. There is no underestimating the work that the ladies' group did over the years, not only in voluntary support but raising money. They were responsible for large contributions of funds for a number of replacement vehicles for the club – they were, at times, a formidable group. The one thing they weren't ever going to do was control our Mr Long. As soon as Steve became uncomfortable with them he would act. Words would be exchanged, maybe a few tears (not from Steve), and then everything would settle down again.

There were some wonderful characters in the ladies' group and some strong ones. Stella was a formidable character and certainly channelled the efforts of the group in the early years. She later went on to become a member of the club's management committee. One of the best loved members of the ladies' group was Gran Towells. Gran, as she was always affectionately known, was the grandmother of Brendan O'Brien, a club member. When Brendan's parents moved from Bedminster Down to the village of Felton, Brendan decided to stay with his Gran in Brooklyn Road, not far from the club. Gran joined the ladies' group around 1971 and helped out in the canteen on junior nights. During the era of the summer cafe, Gran would sit at a table producing meticulously presented salads for the holidaymakers. She couldn't be rushed, no matter what the demand, her salads were presented as a work of art. As Brooklyn Road sat at the bottom of a steep hill, we would pick her up on Tuesday evenings if Brendan wasn't around and drop her home afterwards. She continued to help out at juniors until well after her 80th birthday – she was a wonderful lady, loved by us all.

Many of the ladies served the club for years. They all became part of the greater club family, joining us on evenings out and even holidays. When I took my first junior holiday to Kerne Bridge, I benefited from having Jean and Don Smith with me. Jean was a member of the ladies' group and Don was a helper. Rob 'Smudge' Smith was a member at the time and then became a member of the junior staff when I was running the junior section. Jean would do her stint behind the canteen with Jess Bacon – Friday nights, I think. Chips would be on the menu on a Friday and Don would bring Jean to the club armed with buckets of chipped potatoes that she had prepared earlier at home. The deep fat fryer would billow steam out through the club wall via a specially built vent – this was a step up from salad rolls and hotdogs!

Daphne Evans joined the ladies' group, following her husband, Frank, who originally came to do weightlifting at the club. Frank and Daphne had two daughters, so there wasn't an immediate, obvious link to the club, but they got involved and stayed for years. Daphne and Frank would accompany the club to Cornwall for years, helping with the cooking and supporting those running the holidays. Daphne was a lovely lady who would do anything for the club. She went on to serve as a member of the management committee, staying with the club right to its final days. There always needed to be a head honcho. Grace Chappell filled the role for a number of years. Like many of the group, Grace had sons that had either been members or were members at that time. Geoff had already left the club when Grace got involved, but Andy, her youngest, was a member, and he later performed with Steve as part of a singing cabaret act. Diane Scarborough made an immediate impact on the ladies' group by running off with the best Victoria sandwich sponge cake award in her first summer fayre – what a bloody cheek!

While the ladies' group seemed to be made up of the more mature women from the community early on, that eventually changed as the second breed of helpers dragged their belea-guered girlfriends, and then wives, into the fold. It had to be said that the likes of Diane Scarborough and Sylvia Bratchel were a more pleasing look on the eye and they were probably more tolerant of the antics of the membership. The ladies' group provided a vital source of funding for the club over many years, with many of the club's vehicles being purchased with significant donations from the group. The junior section at one stage was virtually staffed by voluntary ladies. Dave Brace was running the juniors at that time and, while the purists might raise an eyebrow, these ladies were absolutely committed to the role they were playing. Normally there is a catalyst for this sort of occurrence and in this case it was Goretta Thorne, or Gor as we all called her. Gor lived locally and she dragged a couple of her friends along to help out at junior club. I'm sure Dave had his work cut out at times – but you can't argue that it wasn't successful, because it was.

As well as the voluntary staff that evolved from its membership, there were occasions when something out of the ordinary would happen and support would come from an unexpected source.

Steve's regular battles with football teams would provide an unexpected benefit. The Fed had stopped providing football leagues above under-16s. As a consequence, most lads would have to get their football elsewhere. Andy Seer, a helper at the time, suggested we have a senior football team, consisting of club helpers and members over the age of sixteen. The programme at the time would accommodate it and that's what happened. Existing staff helpers like Andy Seer , Esky, Waffler, Ray Davies, Michael 'Tatty' Whitlock all signed, along with those of us who had been hammered all the previous season at under-16s level. There was myself, Alan 'Bill' Burge, Paul 'Olly' Ollis, Brendan O'Brien (who later did an exquisite Shirley Bassey at a club Show Down), Jeff Trought, John Lewis, Tony Cole and Phil 'Dapper' Davies, who was a year younger than most of us but physically equipped for men's football. Ray and Phil were brothers and, in good club tradition, their mum, Lottie, was a member of the ladies' group. As in a lot of brother relationships, things were not always plain sailing when they were on the pitch together and both of them had tempers. Sparks would sometimes fly between them – much to everyone's displeasure – but a source of amusement looking back.

Phil and I were great friends back then. His dad had died suddenly when he was fourteen or fifteen. Lottie had three boys and a daughter. It would have been tough. Phil was my first drinking partner, along with two other members, Jeff Trought and Mervyn Cook. I was the biggest (by quite a few pounds), so we would go down to Bedminster on a Saturday night and we would make for the Tap & Barrel public house. We would venture in and I would be pushed to the front. We were all under age – we were all still at school. Later, we ventured into town, probably at Dapper's suggestion. We chose a pub out of the way. In we went and to our surprise it was quiet for a Saturday night. I wandered up to the bar and ordered while Dapper went to the gents for a leg, thirty seconds later he came hurtling back out of the gents – we had wandered into what was a gay pub. This was 1969, we hadn't had the benefit of a liberated society. We returned to our regular haunt at Bedminster.

The senior football team ran for several years and attracted players from outside of the club community. This was to be a problem for Steve. He had accepted the need for the team; on the basis of it addressing the need for retaining voluntary staff. However, adults from outside of the club presented a different proposition. An agreement was reached, they would have to train and pay club subs to acquire membership status. If they embraced the club ethos they could even become members of the voluntary staff. And some of them did, Timothy and Anthony Butcher, alias Tim and Tony, alias the Butcher Twins, and Tony Fouracres. All of them remained club helpers for many years.

There were adults who ventured into the club to undertake specific activities – for instance Roy James came in as a football coach, Frank Evans came to do weightlifting – dragging his long suffering wife, Daphne, along to help behind the canteen. They would both accompany the members on club holidays, as did the James gang – Roy, wife Jill, Pam, Rachael and Ian. Tony Lainchbury was a local insurance salesman when he became a helper. Most of the helpers that came as adults into the club family were connected to the membership in some way. John Roberts was living locally on Bedminster Down when he became involved with the club and it wasn't long before he dragged his mate, John Hairs, along – and then their wives.

Some of the membership which had drifted away from the club would later return – "Can I help, Steve?" they would ask. It was never a straightforward yes, regardless of our staffing position at the time. Interested individuals were expected to demonstrate their suitability and their commitment in advance. The success of the club largely depended on the relationship between those who were members and those who were helping. Commitment was key to that relationship.

When the decision was taken not to continue with the post of assistant leader, the money was used to pay existing members of voluntary staff.

Having a continuous supply of voluntary staff to support the leader would be a continuing problem over the club's lifetime. The original group had set a very high standard in respect of ability and commitment. The club was vibrant and, at its peak, open seven days a week. While Saturday had always remained a day of closure for general club, a succession of weekend activities would always ensure that staff was going to be required over weekends. For any adult, the commitment of a night a week at the club was commitment enough – but weekends as well? However, many did – for many years.

Most of us old hands ran football teams at some point, although the likes of me, my old mate Barry, Bratch, Mike Palmer and Scarby would probably not put it down as one of our more favourite activities. Many parents did do it, all embracing the club's philosophy when it came to running football teams. There were a whole range of parents who ended up running football teams.

There were a few public appeals for help during Steve's reign and one, I believe, under Russ Cooper's. On the 9 January 1987, four thousand leaflets were delivered to the community asking for help – there wasn't one reply. The club would not have been as successful as it was without the hundreds of voluntary staff that gave their time so willingly over the years. They ran activities, supported holidays, arranged trips, did fundraising, undertook decorating, ran the canteen. They did the lot – and did it for free.

Why did they do it? Well, for many of them you are going to have to ask them yourself. It would be easy to put it down to some great sense of moral responsibility and all that sort of claptrap. But for most, like me, it was down to one thing only – we enjoyed it. For those few that did many years, the challenge was accepting that many things changed along the way. The membership changed, the needs of young people changed and finally, the ethics that had driven the club to its height of success seemingly disappeared.

One thing that was constant was the importance of the relationship between the full-time leader and his staff. Steve certainly wasn't the easiest of people to get along with at times and a few staff left following differences of opinion. I am sure Steve would have reflected on the loss of people like Esky, Sherman, Andy Seer and others years later and thought, "I might have dealt with this better." Steve would, in time, realise that it was better to share a member of the voluntary staff with his girlfriend or wife than not benefit at all from their time. Bratch and Scarby were some of the first members of voluntary staff to integrate their partners into the club. Both had been members, then a part of the voluntary staff team, before doing what comes naturally to most males – finding themselves somebody to share their life with. For them, the club could coexist in their lives and it seemed that Steve had learned to accept it. It was probably a very wise decision as both went on to give years of service to the club. Dave became Treasurer in 1971 and continued in that role to the end. Steve Bratchel, or Bratch to us all, went on to run the junior club for a period as well as being a member of the voluntary staff team for many years. Both remained loyal to the club until the last days.

Social gatherings of the voluntary staff happened during most of the club's existence. Many of the staff were members of the Ex-Service Club adjacent to the club's premises during the 60s and 70s and we would gather there on a Saturday night, or even after club had finished during the week. Rumour has it that the first staff social group consisted of a group that would visit the Kings Cinema in Old Market, late on Friday nights to watch some pretty dodgy films – but it is only rumour! For quite some time a few would gather at the Ex-Service Club on a Saturday before walking around to Andy Seer's home to watch Match of the Day as Andy had a colour television. Queenie, Andy's mother as she was known, always made us very welcome. Another routine involved a walk around the helpers' homes on Christmas morning. The trouble with this was that too many helpers lived in a small area. Starting from Gerry's in Tyntesfield Road, then Seer's, Grimley's, Allen's and Lewis's in Ilchester Crescent, Stacey's in Brooklyn Road and then Lovell's in Lewis Road. Some of us never made it around.

Staff meals and nights out were good events and often focused around music. There were trips to the Webbington Country Club and the Old Granary to see cabaret acts or jazz musicians and social gathering for meals in decent restaurants. Mattie's Restaurant in Bishopsworth was a favourite for many years. It was owned by Ian and Jane Lyons, they became great friends and supporters of the club and provided the food at a number of functions held at the club.

The early success of Show Down had seen the formation of The Down Folk, a singing trio of Steve, Phil 'Pippo' Stacey and Roy Lewis (my dad). The trio would entertain at social clubs and various hotels. Over the years, Steve had a number of groups and individuals that would join him in cabaret and often members of the voluntary staff team would go along in support.

It would be pointless to try and list all the members of the voluntary staff team over the years. There will be some that get more mentions than others in this account; after all it's my book! But I would not decry the right of any of them to say they played a part in the club's history, no more or less than any of us.

7

Juniors

The opening of the junior club in 1966 ensured the premises were full to capacity most evenings a week. When taking over responsibility for juniors in 1972, I had a small but committed staff team. Dave Scarby had been helping out at juniors when Dave Phillips was in charge. I was an apprentice electrical fitter at the time and would have to go to college once a month for a week at a time in Barnstaple. Cover arrangements were put in place.

The first year went as well as I could have hoped for; the second year was to provide greater challenges.

The club membership nearly always came from within the community. There were some notable exceptions. In the early part of 1969, a small group of lads had joined the junior club from Withywood. Not many of them, but enough for Steve and Dave to be concerned whether they would get on with the rest of the membership, which came predominantly from the local area. There was a territorial difference between the areas. I was asked to keep an eye on this new group and help them settle, which I did. It became the start of an influx of members from the Withywood area, which continued until the club's closure. At the start of the club year in September 1973, the junior club was buzzing. We had a full house of one hundred members, sometimes ninety of them attending on a single night. In the midst of this organised mayhem, as it must have seemed looking back, we had another group.

I think the situation just crept up on us running the juniors at the time. I was aware that a certain group of boys were gaining more of my attention than the rest, their activities, both inside and outside, of the club were causing me problems – they were the Headley Park Mob as I labelled them.

We reached an unmanageable level and made a huge decision – to shut junior club for a few weeks. I had discussed the situation with Steve and he was extremely supportive. I wrote to all the parents of the members and explained the reason for the decision. Instead of opening the club for the membership, we would meet as a staff team on both nights. I needed more staff to help out. Steve agreed.

I went to the senior membership for assistance. Now, if you have ever been in a situation like this you would want to think that it would be the more responsible membership that would come to the rescue. Well, let's just say there was a mixture! Kevin 'Hicks' Hickery and Bob Cook were two of the members that volunteered. Hicks was probably one of the most challenging members we had around at that time. He had an alliance with Paul Hawker, or Hawkman as he was called. This alliance had brought mayhem to the community on a number of occasions – Hicks and Hawkman were legendary! Fact or myth – well you will have to ask them! Cooky was Hicks' neighbour and could be a bloody pain in the ass at times. These two lads had volunteered to help and along they came – attending all the training sessions. Those lads, along with the ones that came later – Paul Havill, Bob Smith, Martin Skidmore, Pete Windell, Neil Bacon, were inspirational. Without wishing to embarrass Paul, our first meeting was less auspicious. Steve had asked me to give him a hand one night to deal with a senior member who was led across the chairs in his office the worse for wear from alcohol a bottle of Scotsmac, which is a blend of whiskey and wine. In short, this poor lad, who was probably around fourteen years of age, was out of it. We got him home safely and during the months that followed I learned more about him. He became a junior member of staff, supported me on several junior club holidays and we remain great friends to this day.

The Headley Park Mob brought me new challenges. They were pack hunters – always in a group. They would follow the same route to club most weeks, much to the displeasure of every resident that had a greenhouse. One lad was a year older than the rest – Mark 'Jolly' Jones. Jolly was tall with flame red hair – he stuck out. There was his brother Nick, the two Presses – Derek and Philip, the two Beers – Dave and Colin, Mike Bull and Wayne Shiner. Poor Jolly always seemed to be getting the blame for the greenhouse effect, even though I'm pretty sure he wasn't always the main protagonist. Beneath what seemed a hard exterior there was something else. Communication was going to be the key ingredient to building a working relationship with this group. Nearly forty years later, I still believe that communication is the key to most relationships. At work, I do sometimes get asked "where did you get your management skills?" (I assume that's complimentary). "I learned it working with young people at BDBC, where if you couldn't communicate you would fail miserably," I would reply. The likes of Jolly Jones and the Headley Park Mob was where I learned my trade.

The problems I experienced with the group resulted in me being on first name terms with many of their parents. Most of them lived in a small area within a corner of Headley Park, tucked away opposite the local junior school. All the parents of the group knew one another, well most of them anyway. They lived just around the corner from each other. The Beers, Jones and Presses would remain the focus of my attention for many years in the junior club. The parents were always very understanding, "We really do appreciate what you do at the club, Lou," they would say. I found myself even tracking them down at the Maytree Pub, where they all drank for a while.

Working with a small group at the club could have its

rewards. Sometimes it was difficult to balance the issues for these young people against your own experiences growing up at a similar age. I worked with many challenging youngsters at the club, yes, even some disturbed ones. This group from Headley Park was just hard work for a while. I ran several junior holidays under my tenure, Kerne Bridge, the Lake District and Lyme Regis – they always came and gave us all some of the most memorable moments, one way or another.

In later years I would work with another set of Jones' at the club, this time the sons of Jolly.

The influx of new staff gave us the impetus we needed at the time, not a case of re-taking the streets, but more a case of re-gaining control of the canteen. I am not sure whether Steve was convinced that the new staff would be able to deliver. But deliver they did, they were loyal, committed, and reliable. Yes, some of them did have a different approach and I am not sure that their style would fit into any youth workers' manual at the time. But we got by and came out the other side.

It would be easy to assume that my time as junior leader was challenging and, yes, there were moments that were difficult. However, it was probably one of my most rewarding periods – I had a brilliant time.

Older members would provide the backbone for running the junior club for the rest of the club's life. Tony Frost, one of the first members in 1964, fulfilled the role for a while. Steve Bratchel did for years and so did Dave Brace. In Dave's reign, there was a significant change as most of his helpers were in fact ladies and damn good they were as well. Dave was an enigmatic character and did a good job, nurturing the junior club during the height of Russ's reign as leader – I'm sure a challenge for them both. The last of the junior leaders was Shaun Gould. I would put Shaun up there with the best of youth workers I ever worked alongside.

8

Governance

While the governing body of the club will always be reported as the club's own parliament, there was a constitutional requirement for the club to have a management committee. Steve was not a great lover of having anything imposed on him but, one assumes, that as he was only twenty-three years old when he was appointed, he wasn't going to kick up a fuss over the management committee he had inherited. Well, not at first anyway.

The original management committee when the club opened in the new building was the same group that had overseen the construction of the new building. Its chairman was Stephen Kew, a local solicitor, and then there was Ted Thorne, Steve Steven, John Leader, and a few local dignitaries and Rotarians – that's the way it was back then. Steve's relationship with the chairman was strained, especially after an early summoning of our new leader to the offices of Tuckett, Williams & Kew. Steve was kept waiting, he didn't like being controlled.

Eventually, many of the original committee were replaced. Andy Seer became the first elected members' representative to the committee and then the likes of Roy Lewis and Bill Player were added, followed by Paul Allen and Chris Sherman. True to later form, Steve wanted a management committee of his choosing. Eventually Paul became secretary, and Chris became chairman. However, what Steve failed to realise was that these individuals would have lives outside of the club and the support they had provided as unattached single men would be unsustainable when the pressures of careers and partners developed. However, he did get the treasurer he wanted. It would be years later that Steve eventually got the type of chairman he so wanted – his name was David Baker.

Stephen Truman Long, giving him his full-name, was never a lover of authority. By his own admission, he wasn't the best of pupils at school and had a fractious relationship with his father. The early management committee of the club typically reflected the groups that were in the same positions in other clubs at the time – professional people from industry, commerce and professional organisations across the city. There were always representatives from the Youth Service or the City Council and the Bristol Federation of Boys' Clubs (as it was at the time). Bert Wilcox was a city councillor, Chris Wilcox was the general secretary at the Fed, Stephen Kew was a solicitor. They would all arrive in suits and ties for their meeting at the club, unless the meeting had been moved to the offices of Tuckett, Williams & Kew, in Small Street, in the city. I remember attending these offices as the members' representative on one occasion – Stephen Kew sat in a high-backed black leather chair – Christ, what an ego! Mr Kew tried to control Mr Long – Mr Long was not going to have that. There's no doubt that having well-connected people on your management committee helped. Rotarians and businessmen had connections to money, and money would always be needed.

A strong leader and resolute voluntary staff group in the early years provided the foundation that would see the club through the rest of its lifetime.

The evolution of the club's parliament in 1969 was to change the club forever. I was lucky enough to be one of the group of members that sat in the club's quiet room on that Sunday evening when Steve explained the whole meaning of self-governance. I had no concept of what would then follow

Parliament in operation

and how that decision would ultimately impact on me for the rest of my life. Looking back now, I struggle to remember who was at that meeting or how many of us were there. I remember quite clearly it took place on a Sunday night at the club and there were around thirty of us. The background to that meeting is recalled by Dave Scarborough: "The meeting was to discuss a platform to formalise the discussions that regularly happened in the club's Thames van to or from trips. The members' committee had become irrelevant." Those who attended had just received a typed note from Steve asking us to attend. Whether he felt that this was an opportune moment or whether it was part of a longer-term plan I am not sure. Certainly the club was booming and there was, on reflection, an energy building from within that wanted to be part of something different. From that point on, our small boys' club in a little corner of Bedminster Down developed to be one of the leading youth organisations in the country. Some, even from the outside, would say it was the best in the country, outstanding and above the performance of the rest. Even a visit by Her Majesty's Inspectorate in 1989, described it as a leading example. I would say that, yes, it probably did show the light in members' participation and empowerment – but I'm biased and always will be.

That Sunday night's discussion was based on our attempt to create an open-democracy at the club. This ultimately resulted in the following:

A) A parliament which gathers monthly.

B) An equipment group which meets once a week.

Steve's relationship with parliament was interesting. This was his baby, it's what he passionately believed in, it's what he practiced and lauded about. However, it wasn't always plain sailing. Editions of Democracy, the document regularly produced at the end of each club year by Steve that recorded all the discussions at parliament, still make interesting reading years later. Democracy recorded parliament's discussions on one side of the page and then Steve's thoughts on the meeting on the other. For those adults who attended regular parliament meetings over the years, we experienced a range of emotions from inspirational to exasperating and ultimately disillusion – working with young people could be frustrating at times.

Steve's concept of parliament was based on the book Summerhill by AS Neill. (Summerhill School was founded in 1921. It is a democratic, self-governing school in which the adults and children have equal status. The daily life of the school is governed by the school meetings, usually held twice a week in which everybody has an equal vote.)

Parliament was the opportunity for the members of the club to have their say and, importantly, make the key decisions on how their club was to operate. As always, there were occasions when small peer groups would attempt to coerce the membership into making the decisions that they wanted. They rarely succeeded and on the occasions that they did, those decisions would be subject to scrutiny of the next parliament (the following month). The range of topics that were discussed over the years would be too long to list – but some of them are worth mentioning.

The Great Toilet Paper debate is legendary in the club's history, and was one of the subjects Steve wrote about (Soft & Hard, by STL). When it opened in 1964, it had acquired boxes and boxes of toilet paper from a local hotel – probably The Grosvenor. It was the single-leaf tracing paper type which required holders on the wall. These holders were regularly filled from this seemingly endless supply of replacements from the club's store cupboard. It went on for years until during one parliament the question from the floor was "can we have softer toilet paper?" It was discussed and agreed. However it wasn't acted on by the membership. Some two years later, a representative from HMI (Her Majesty's Inspectors) asked if they could attend parliament. We often had guests, or dignitaries, who had asked if they could attend parliament to witness the proceedings. Their attendance at the respective parliament was always discussed in advance and sanctioned by the group at the time. On this particular occasion, it was one of Her Majesty's Inspectors. One of the members present suddenly recalled the debate of two years previous – and the discussion commenced again. Steve explained that at the present rate of consumption, we had about ten years of stock. The debate followed with some of the members explaining that their use of the toilets was being restricted by the presence of the stuff. "It doesn't so much clean as smudge," was one comment. Her Majesty's Inspector sat po-faced as the rest of the assembly giggled joyously.

The member who had raised the subject explained that he had done his homework and could get the soft paper at the Co-op. Others said it would be better to buy in bulk, so maybe Tesco, or Cash & Carry, where Steve gets the sweets.

They also explained that the endless pile of the hard stuff could be sold at the club's Christmas Fayre. And so it happened – new toilet roll holders were purchased to accommodate the new supply but Steve installed them next to the existing holders. Hence, when new prospective members were shown around and viewed the cubicles – "Look, you even have a choice of toilet paper – soft or hard." And Her Majesty's Inspector was suitably impressed.

On the 18 November 1983, there was an emergency parliament. The week before had been Club Week, the week when we undertake our annual house-to-house collection. At this annual event, members would collect pre-delivered envelopes, which allowed the community to make cash donations to the club. A neighbour had come to the club and explained that two opened Club Week envelopes had been found behind her hedge.

Additionally, at about 11pm on the night of the collection, an elderly lady who had been a supporter of the club for years received a knock on the door from two boys, who said they were from the club. She was over eighty years old at the time and had been a supporter of the club for forty-two years. They wanted money – she refused and went to her phone. They ran.

An emergency parliament was called and forty members attended. All the details were provided to the members.

There haven't been many occasions during my time at the club when the adults attending parliament were asked to leave the room – this was one of those occasions. On our return, we were informed that four boys had been identified who had been responsible for the opened envelopes – two were at the meeting and two weren't.

There was outrage from the membership regarding the other matter. Retribution would have resulted if the boys responsible would have been club members or school colleagues. Over the weeks that followed, Steve became more confident that these individuals hadn't been club members, although the fact they were aware of the lady's support of the club and the fact that it was Club Week must have come from within the organisation.

The lads responsible for stealing went to see the club leader, succumbing to the pressure from their mates and were dealt with internally.

Some fourteen years after the club had moved to self-governance, an evolving membership was as passionate as ever about their club. They would protect it from attack, whether from inside or out – nobody would be allowed to tarnish the name of the club that they loved.

From 1969 onwards, parliament would make all the key decisions at the club. Whether it was the purchasing of an adventure centre in South Wales, a new club van, the cost of subs to the range and duration of gym sessions. It would deal with stealing on the odd occasions that it happened and, yes, it did discuss the girls issue. There were times when the outlook of parliament looked bleak. In STL's notes on the parliament (see Democracy 10) held on the 23 February 1987 he wrote: "This was a watershed in the history of our parliaments. Possibly the most disastrous one we've ever had and really causing us all to stop and look and think." (ref: Turn the Tele Off, Stu)

On the 24 April 1987 he wrote: "So we go on, but the truth is that the club is at its unhappiest and its democracy is at its most unrealistic in its history."

The atmosphere within the club could change, even sometimes during one night. I believe this was sometimes due to a continually evolving membership. Periods when the club was at its vibrant best were when the members themselves were the active types that embraced the club's philosophy and were determined to make the best use of the facilities and the culture. Often these groups would be the backbone of the membership through which most things were energised. However, it was possible to get a small group that changed the atmosphere at will, even without knowing. While the Headley Park Mob had created a great challenge to me when I was running the junior club, these kids were only juniors.

By the time they had got to seniors they were largely different and certainly didn't operate as a pack as they had at juniors. There were small groups and individuals that presented the club with difficulties over the years and they could disrupt the normal proceedings – especially meetings like parliament.

In December 1981, such a powerhouse existed – three senior members. Rumours were rife; this group had indicated that there needed to be two major changes to the club. Firstly, that girls needed to be admitted and secondly, the leader, Steve Long, needed to be replaced.

And so on Friday 4 December 1981, the club's parliament sat down and Steve, aware of the rumours, said his piece. The question was asked, "Did the membership have faith in its leader?" Even now recalling it over thirty years later, it's incredible – as adults we were there to provide a service to the members – but was it the type of service that the membership wanted? Well, in the end it must have been as thirty-eight out of the forty that attended that parliament were in favour of a Vote of Confidence in their leader, with two abstentions. And the key protagonist – well, as you would expect, he didn't turn up.

For Steve, did he find it humiliating? No. "I am answerable you see, to the clients. Not to some well-meaning managing body, or indeed to an even more distant hierarchy of professional youth officers and the like," he stated. (Ref: Democracy 5/6.)

The girls' debate didn't go away and at the next parliament in February the girls' issue was discussed again – the members said no and the club moved on. Over the many years of my involvement, there had been many debates and discussions around the girls' issue. The National Association of Boys' Clubs was formed in 1925 and grew rapidly. The creation of the new premises for Bedminster Down Boys' Club in the early 1960s was in line with the thinking both nationally and locally. What probably wasn't anticipated was the strength and stature of the boys' club in South Bristol. I actually never knew anyone at Bedminster Down who was against the principle of there being facilities for girls on Bedminster Down. The issue was, and would always be, could, or should, they be accommodated within the boys' club premises and at what expense? Faced with a membership of 250 and the premises being packed every night, it would have been difficult to suggest that the building was underused. Any inclusion of girls would have had a direct impact on the existing membership and they were unlikely to let that happen – which is why the various debates that did happen always returned the same answer from the membership – No. There will always be those who argue that the members' decision could be influenced by the opinions of the adults around them. That's true, it could have been – but it wasn't. And let us remember that the pressure for BDBC to change came from adults – those adults who always thought that they knew what was in the best interests of those young people they deemed to represent. There was never, as far as I am aware, any huge demand from the girls on the estate to use the facilities. However, the whole issue of girls being allowed in was to never go away and the consequences would eventually be devastating.

Steve's despair at those last parliaments of the 1986 – 87 club year seemed long gone by end of the first parliament when the club opened again in September 1987. "A fine start to the season. A promising omen for this year perhaps." (Ref: Democracy 11.)

Parliament would continually challenge a lot of the membership over the years. For many it was a unique opportunity to get involved in the running of their club, for others it was a distraction from doing what they wanted to do – go in the gym, play snooker, etc.

When Steve announced his retirement in January 1990, it would be parliament, the membership, that would ultimately take responsibility for appointing its new club leader. Grey suits had been replaced with sweat-shirts, age by youth, and experience by learning. Empowerment at its best.

While there will always be those cynics who doubted the credibility of parliament – even its wisdom – it was undoubtedly youth work at its very best. For me, I attended many parliaments as a member and as an adult. It taught me the true meaning of democracy and empowerment – and that would have an impact on me for the rest of my life.

9

Drama

Musical theatre had a big impact on Steve Long growing up, so it should be no surprise that drama would feature significantly within its programme.

The club's Show Down was the annual Christmas production. The first show was performed on Thursday 16 December 1965 to an invited guest list of local elderly people and then again to a ticket-paying audience on the following two nights. Too young to be a member, I sat in the audience on the Friday night.

The members had dragged some railway sleepers from Zion Methodist Church around to the club to form the base of the stage and a scaffold was erected at the back from which Ivor Bennett would precariously hang – operating the limited number of spotlights. The cast was an intriguing mixture – Chris Sherman, Andy Seer, Roger Grimley, Bob Lewington, Terry Windows (as a tramp), Wiggle Sollars – they all mucked in, hamming around to provide entertainment for the locals. Chris' performance as the mad club leader, being harangued by Mike 'Tatty' Whitlock, will never be forgotten by me. The first Ballet Los Trios of Wiggle, Remould and Roachy (Pete Sollars, Steve Raines and Mike Roach) was outstanding. Some of the sketches performed in the first year would be repeated over the years to come – a different cast and a different audience – but the same laughs. The first half closed with a camp fire scene and the cast singing *Where Have All the Flowers Gone?* And the end of the second half closed with a traditional Christmas scene – the cast dressed in Victorian cloaks and holding lanterns. To accompany the show, a glossy Show Down programme had been produced courtesy of Ted Thorne, a member of the management committee.

That first Show Down of 1965 was to set the standard for what was to follow.

There were some legendary performances over the years that followed. Dave Scarborough as Whispering Paul McDowell, fronting The Temperance Seven, Wiggle, Remould and Roachy changing their ballet clothes to become The Beverley Sisters. The outstanding Wilson, Keppel and Betty routine undertaken by Remould, Leggy and Geoff Chappell in 1967 was derived from the leader's love of theatre. The 1967 show also introduced the audience to the club's love of Cornish folk music, with the haunting *It's as Dark as a Dungeon*, performed by the cast to open the second half and the traditional Christmas scene being replaced by a Cornish folk scene to close the show. Brendan O'Brien as Shirley Bassey in 1968, making a guest appearance to accompany the return of The Temperance Seven.

If I remember anything from that early show, it would be the willingness of the members to expose themselves to the stage and bright lights in a selection of mad sketches. Young adult leaders were prepared to dress in mad costumes, some as women, vicars, tramps, ballet dancers without any noticeable qualms. They even sang Christmas carols. A year later, I was a member and I stood on stage for my first Show Down – December 1966 – a version of The Beatles' *Yellow Submarine*. Each year the boundaries were pushed a little further but the format remained the same. The first night was the club giving back to the community it served and loved. Transport was provided for those elderly people who would struggle to get to the club under their own steam. Guests were welcomed to the evening with a glass of sherry and provided with a plated buffet at half-time. All the members were involved. We showed people to their seats, helped them to the toilets, got them teas and coffees and entertained them on the stage. When the lights dimmed and the words of *Old Rugged Cross* floated from the stage, the audience fell silent and tears would well in the eyes of many of our senior citizens.

Show Down quickly became a tradition at the club – yes, there were years when finding a cast or the material proved a bit more challenging and even one year when Steve announced that there would be no more Show Downs – but the membership responded, as they always did. New material was found and off we went again. In 1969, Steve decided that he would like to produce some extracts from Lionel Bart's *Oliver*, which he had seen in the West End, using members of the junior club. Whether it was my likeness in size to Harry Secombe that made Steve ask me to play the role of Bumble – enter Dave 'Scarby' again: "Sun blazing through the gym windows as we set up the cafe. Andy Lou let rip with 'Who will buy this wonderful morning?' Alison Cook responded with 'I wish someone would'. Priceless."

On the 27 March 1969, *Oliver*, BDBC fashion, premiered at the club's Open Night where the guest of honour was Stratford Johns, an actor famous for playing the role of Inspector Barlow in the BBC's Production of Z Cars and Softly, Softly. *Oliver* was the club's first attempt at serious musical drama and will always be remembered for the performances of Keith Gregory, cast as Oliver. Nobody knew Keith could sing until the rehearsals and could he sing! The complication for me was that as the success of *Oliver* grew so did requests for performances. I was living in Devon during the week, my first year of an apprenticeship with the then-Central Electricity Generating Board, and only got home occasionally. So Esky, who was originally cast as Mr Bumble's assistant would play my role in my absence and Jeff Cox would play his assistant. For its debut at Show Down in

1969, it was the combination of Gerald and Brendan O'Brien in the role – which is why the photographs taken at the time have the costumes being worn by different people.

Following that Open Night, Steve took *Oliver* to a number of social clubs and it was also performed at the 1969 Show Down with the brilliant Chris Sherman as Fagin. However, it will always be the performance at The Granary Club in Bristol that will be remembered most of all. The Granary was a frequent haunt of Steve, staff and some of the senior members – to hear the jazz bands. It was a loud, drinking club. On the night the club performed *Oliver*, when Keith Gregory sang the first notes of *Where is Love?* the whole place came to a halt. The ovation was incredible and the great Humphrey Littleton was there to witness it all.

And so musical drama came to Bedminster Down Boys' Club. The club moved quickly from *Oliver* to *Trust Us*, an original drama written by the members – yes, us! I was a member of the cast, the oldest one.

Buoyed by the success of *Oliver*, Steve decided he would introduce members to the theatre and the West End. I went on trips to see Hair and Jesus Christ Superstar – sometimes using the children's home in Cuffley as our base. I remember the visit to see Hair quite vividly because outside the theatre front doors was a group from the Hare Krishna Mantra performing – and so we all joined in. There is a wonderful personal postscript of our trip to see *Hair*. The visit was the start of my love of musical theatre which is still as strong today. So blown away was I with Hair that I immediately went out and bought the album (vinyl in those days). Now, Daddy could be a bit of a prude, especially when it came to bad language – and I certainly didn't benefit from any great sex education lessons. Royston (Daddy) was obviously intrigued with this Hair thing, as it was topic of conversation at the club at the time (songs about sex and naked people prancing about on the stage) but resisted the temptation to

One of the many show rehearsals

ask me about it. However, we only had one record player (for playing vinyl) and that was in the lounge or front room as it was called in those days. Well, I trotted off to bed late one night and just as I was about to nod off, could hear the music from Hair being played downstairs. So I got up, crept down the stairs and was just about to push open the front-room door when a track about masturbation echoed out of the front room. I would have loved to have seen my father's face but I retreated upstairs quickly and never found out how much of the album he actually listened to.

Anyway, Steve was hoping, I'm sure, to energise his membership into musical theatre. It was following the visit to see JCS in March 1972 that the concept of *Trust Us* was born. An interested group was put together and we sat down to work on the script and the songs. We wrote down the issues affecting us at the time. I was the oldest member in the cast, included, I'm sure in part, by Steve to exercise some influence and control over the antics of some of the characters in the cast. The age range was quite noticeable, with the youngest ones being Bob Smith and Neil Bacon. Any group that included 'Hicks' in the midst was going to be interesting. Also in the cast was Leonard Scotland, our only black member at the time. We tackled football hooliganism, drinking, racism and smoking using a variety of songs with or without the right lyrics. Steve pulled in Bob Elliot to help with the rehearsals. Bob was National Association of Boys' Clubs Regional Officer at the time and had an office in Dunn's Buildings, home of the Fed. There were twenty of us in the cast.

Publicity shot for *Turn the Tele off Stu* 1987

Trust us 1972

Who Cares 1981

Bristol Hippodrome Show 1985 – Wiggle, Dougie and Lou

The old boys rehearsing for the second Bristol Hippodrome Show 1989

There seems little point in relaying again the success of *Trust Us*. Yes, it's worth noting for the record that it eventually went on to win the Bill Owen Award for best all-Male cast and the Olivier Award for the best piece of drama at the NABC's National Drama Festival at the University of Reading on the 15 July 1972. But it's also worth noting that all of us had a ball along the way. We didn't set out, I am sure, with any expectations of success – why would we? We had no benchmark of what success was. We were an inarticulate group that just got on. When I look at some of the photographs taken during rehearsals, it's obvious we were enjoying ourselves. So to you all, if you ever get to read this, my thanks – Gary, Chilly, Shammy, Hicks, Bratch, Smudge, Geoff, Beano, Mitch, Jimmer, Lenny, Ross, Jonesy, Stevie T, Paul, Neil, Shaun, Mark, Kinger and John F. Little did you know at the time that *Trust Us* would be the benchmark for the rest to aspire to.

And so, the little club in a corner of Bedminster Down had once again hit the headlines. The BBC filmed a ten-minute slot of *Trust Us* on location around the area – even a session at Ashton Gate, the home of Bristol City Football Club.

The club continued to provide musical dramas written by the membership until 1986. In 1977, it was Albert Skinner. In 1981, it was *Who Cares?* In 1983 it was *Mid-Summers Day's Nightmare* and in 1986 it was *Turn the Tele off, Stu*. They were all unique and produced stunning performances from a number of club members like Doug Riddiford, Alan Dogget, Mike Burton and Mike Calloway. Many of those members involved in those productions went on to join a variety of local theatre groups. None of these lads had any drama training before they got involved with their local boys' club. The issues raised by them during the productions were real to them and they found a way to articulate their frustrations about the society they were living in through drama.

What is really difficult to put into context so many years

later is the significance of all these pieces of drama. When you have continued success there becomes expectancy that this is normal. However, all these productions were undertaken with largely different groups of members – the only things that remained constant were the club (including its leader) and its culture. Understanding that, hopefully, allows us to understand the significance that this establishment had on its membership over a sustained period of time.

Many of the shows were filmed by the BBC and they all received national recognition. The saddest thing of all is that probably the frustrations shown by all of them at the time still exist. Is society really willing to learn from the experience of our youth? Probably not!

As well as the numerous stage productions produced by the club, the members found themselves performing at the Bristol Hippodrome on two momentous occasions in 1985 and 1989.

In 1985, Steve hired the Bristol Hippodrome – it was a personal ambition of his to perform on the Hippodrome stage, so what better way to do that than book the place yourself? Steve had a passion for singing and had spent years entertaining at social clubs and elderly people's homes. This had gathered momentum from the first Show Downs, when he, along with Phil 'Pippo' Stacey, Geoff Chappell and Roy Lewis (yes, my father), had entertained the audience as a singing quartet. The Down Folk were formed and the three of them (Geoff opted out), became entertainers. Over the years the faces changed, the numbers changed – but Steve remained constant. Singing was a tradition at the club, especially at Christmas shows and holidays. Summer holidays in Cornwall and Whitsun Camps at Velvet Bottom in Cheddar would not have been the same without the singing.

The origin of the club's love of singing can be found in a small Cornish folk club. The story is that Chris Sherman slipped off one night during the club's first Cornwall looking for a local folk club. He found The Count House and inside he came across Brenda Wootton and her singing partner at the time, John the Fish. The rest, as they say, is history.

Pippo and Esky would take their guitars on the holidays and around the campfire at Cheddar or on the beaches of Cornwall, we would sing. I'm not saying the singing was good or always in tune – but sing we did.

Anyway, back to the Hippodrome. Our success with musical drama had resulted in the club forming a friendship with a number of celebrities. In 1985, it was Bill Owen and Leslie Crowther. Bill said he would join the show and bring Kathy Staff along. They would do a sketch based on the Compo and Nora Batty characters from The Last of the Summer Wine. Leslie said he would compère the whole thing. The show sold out within days. The kids did sketches, the Gaiety Girls (dance group) had a slot, the Old Boys did a re-work of Ballet Los Trios (that was Dougie, Wiggle and me) and Steve sang. At the end, the audience provided a standing ovation. For those who were involved, it was memorable. Our rehearsals for the ballet had taken place on Sunday evenings in the gym at the club. Wiggle had been one of the original cast when it was first performed at the Show Down in 1965. I was in the cast when it was re-produced with a different routine in 1968 . Dougie had been the star of Albert Skinner. The rehearsals had been going reasonably well and Steve had asked his old friend John Scully to cast his eye over our routine. We all knew John from Fry Club, where Steve and his group regularly played. I'm not sure who it was that decided we ought to add a prop to the routine. "How about a tyre?" was all I heard. Tyre? We ended up with a bloody great tractor tyre that Wiggle and I humped around the stage as the female dancers. Dougie, in black ballet tights, was the male. If you witnessed it, I hope you enjoyed it. Only if you were a member of Bedminster Down Boys' Club could you ever think that there is nothing wrong with putting on a ballet tutu and white ballet tights at thirty-two years of age and then dancing in front of 2,000 people at the Bristol Hippodrome.

My involvement in the 1989 show was probably more demanding and I wasn't even performing. Steve announced to the media in early October of 1988 that, to celebrate twenty-five years of the club in its premises in Winford Grove, he was taking Show Down to the Bristol Hippodrome on the 30 April 1989 – the second time the club had taken over the Bristol theatre. The press were told and the story appeared in the local newspapers on the 13 October 1989 but Steve was holding a secret that only a few people knew. He had been diagnosed with a heart condition and needed surgery. His condition appeared to have deteriorated over many months. When he returned from the club's holiday the previous summer, he had confessed it had. The same week as the news conference, Steve asked me to meet him at his home and we sat down to discuss his health. He explained that the condition had got worse and the surgery he needed was imminent. Would I look after the club during his absence?

At a staff meeting held at the club a few days later, I was appointed as one of the paid part-time assistant leaders and twenty-four hours later, Steve advised the rest of the staff team that he was going to be off work for a while and I had the reins. On the 20 October he issued a statement to the membership. He anticipated being off work for three months.

And so, in a period of a week or so, I had taken on the responsibility of heading up the team of paid and voluntary staff that were running the club and somehow had to co-ordinate the Hippodrome show, including the rehearsals. We had also planned, and were in the process of producing, a magazine to celebrate the club's 25th Anniversary at Winford Grove, later to be called *Images*.

Once again, Steve had secured the support of two celebrities, Leslie Crowther and Gary Wilmot. Oh, and to add to the scenario, he had decided there would be two shows on the day at the Hippodrome – so he threw in a matinee!

History will detail that twenty-five kids were in the cast for the show, with a hundred of them on stage for the finale. The Gaiety Girls did their bit and Dougie arranged the Old Boys' sketch – the rumble from West Side Story.

There was a four-year period between these historic shows at the Hippodrome; the likes of which I feel will never be seen again. This young man from Barton Hill had taken the club he loved to the absolute pinnacle of success.

For me, the lead up to the show was demanding. I had taken over the reins from Steve in the previous October. I had two part-time assistants, Mike Palmer and Sean Chaffey, and Steve Bratchel was running the junior club. I didn't feel, at the time, that Mike and Sean were best pleased with my appointment. They had been in post for some time and probably felt overlooked by Steve. I set about pulling the collective team together and started by prioritising what we could do in Steve's absence and what we couldn't. I had a mix of staff, both paid and unpaid and in quality. My role was to just hold the fort until Steve returned – well, that's what I thought at the time.

I am sure Steve thought that he would have his operation and then would slowly return to pick up where he left off, which included putting on the second Hippodrome show. However, the recovery period was longer than he anticipated and his visits to the club were restricted to two hours on a Sunday evening to oversee some of the rehearsals. I would spend what time I could at the club in the morning or afternoon – between jobs as a self-employed electrician. Most of my evenings were spent at the club.

Telephone calls during the mornings increased, whether it was in connection with the show, enquiries about Steve's health or the many other aspects of running an organisation with 250 young people as members. We drafted Marcia

Scully in to help with the selling of the Hippodrome tickets, Gor became a part-time secretary and we employed a new cleaner – Maureen Farr. The only thing I didn't have to worry about was the dealing with the cash the club generated, as the treasurer, Dave Scarborough (Scarby to us all), would come in regularly and cash up. All the staff had to do was put the money in the safe. We had a few part-time clerical assistants over the years, or secretaries. When the club had been at its busiest, we had secured funding for part-time clerical help. I always thought the concept of Steve sitting down and dictating a letter for the secretary to type and then them giving it back to check a bit bizarre, if that's what happened. Steve didn't like being controlled. As in the case with the ladies' group, he was also a perfectionist – recipe for a disaster, I would have thought. Anyway, I didn't need a perfectionist – I needed someone to help me with the administration, take telephone messages and be supportive. Gor fitted the bill on all counts and she even learned to type (well, sort of).

Images, the magazine, was produced to celebrate twenty-five years of the club at Winford – with Scarby doing all the chasing up of the articles. The idea of the magazine had been agreed before Steve had gone off sick. We asked as many people as we could who had a connection with the club to send us their thoughts and include a photo. It seemed a relatively simple project, well it did at the time – if it hadn't been for Scarby it wouldn't have got finished. We had a few periodicals in the club's history with The Key being the most famous one. Put together by senior member, Bob Lewington, just after the club opened in its new premises in 1964, it was well constructed, had reports on a whole number of sporting activities and also included articles on the history of Bedminster Down and first aid hints.

The reviews of the show in the press were glowing. All the money raised was split between the two nominated charities of our guests, Leslie and Gary. In the twenty-five year period since it moved into its new premises, the club had gone from performing annual Christmas shows, to producing four national award-winning drama productions and two sell-out concerts at the Bristol Hippodrome.

10

Celebrities

While Gary Wilmot and Leslie Crowther became supporters and visitors to the club, they weren't the only celebrities to walk through the doors.

Our early management committee was well-connected, especially through the sporting world. There were visits from Stan Cullis (Wolverhampton Wanderers manager), John Mortimore (England International cricketer), Bill Redwood (England International rugby player), Fred Ford (Bristol City manager), Harry Dolman (Bristol City chairman), Jimmy Hill (Coventry City manager) Don Rogers (Swindon Town footballer), Precious McKenzie (British and Commonwealth weightlifting champion), Terry Cooper (Bristol City manager and former England International). Then, there were the TV celebrities and musicians: Stratford Johns (actor), Frankie Vaughan (singer), Fred Wedlock (singer, songwriter), Adge Cutler (singer), Dave Prowse (actor), Acker Bilk (musician), Bill Owen (actor), Jimmy Edwards (actor). The Duke of Beaufort and the Duke of Kent were from our Royal Heritage.

Over the years, there was an endless stream of local celebrities from sport and TV that would willingly come to the club for events, shows, open nights, or pure and simple – just to visit. The club's reputation made it reasonably easy to attract many sportsmen from the local professional clubs, City and Rovers, Bristol Rugby Club and Gloucestershire Cricket Club. We often pushed the boat out to try and entice more nationally recognised celebrities, with some success. The problem always seemed to be matching the availabilities of those people with the club's programme.

One noticeable success was securing Frank Bruno to attend the club's Open Night. Frank had fought Mike Tyson for the World Heavyweight title earlier that year and his popularity was huge. Steve had been trying to get Frank to the club for a number of years and it was ironic that, when he did actually come, Steve was off sick. I was at work when I received the phone call. "Andy, I have a Laura Bruno on the phone for you, can you take the call?" It was Pat, on the works switchboard I think. I have to admit that I was a tad confused in the seconds this was all registering in my mind. It was late on a Friday evening and I was thinking about the weekend. Anyway, Laura explained that she was aware that we had been trying to get Frank to come to the club for a long time (I nodded – stupid isn't it, perhaps she was psychic), he had never been to Bristol – so he thought he would take us up on the offer. And then those final words that would leave me speechless – "Next Wednesday okay?" – 12 July 1989.

We discussed the arrangements including how he would get to Bristol. "Do you mind picking him up please?" she went on. "Oh, and what car will it be, as somebody last year arrived in a Mini to pick him up?" she said giggling. I promised her it wouldn't be a Mini – although I didn't know what it would be at that time. So, we had a date – how the hell I was going to make all the necessary arrangements in such a short-time I had no idea and, to make matters worse, I was getting married in two weeks' time. The further irony about this visit was that Frank was the British public's favourite sports personality, everyone loved him and everyone wanted to meet him. So, with all the offers he was getting, it was inconceivable that this little Boys' Club tucked away in a South Bristol council estate could have secured his services – so the media thought anyway because I couldn't convince anyone that he was coming. Repeated calls to the press and TV (both channels) were unanswered. Or worse, "Thanks for the message we will get back to you." Or, "If he does turn up, let us know." I was bloody flabbergasted – there was one exception – Radio Bristol. Roger Bennett was a very popular Radio Bristol presenter (and a very good musician). He also happened to be Jill James brother, Roy James's wife. Jill was a great friend of the club, as were all her family. I rang her and within minutes I was taking a call from Roger. He was typically generous. "We have a young news reporter at Radio Bristol, Andy. It would be a great coup for him – are you happy with that?" I was more than happy. A local taxi company called Z Cars provided a chauffeur limousine free of charge and we drove up to Frank's home in Essex to pick him up. Yes, I did get some strange looks going up the motorway sprawled out in the back of this white stretch limo – especially when we stopped at the services for a coffee and the driver opened the door for me. We drove to Frank's house and Laura welcomed me in and introduced her young family. I have to say that she was absolutely charming and pretty normal.

Frank was impressed with the car and, apart from stopping on the services on the way back to get him a bag of crisps, the journey was pretty uneventful. He wasn't a great conversationalist and spent his time signing autographs on bits of card to hand out. I knew there was going to be an issue with timing and I was right. You have to give yourself time on a near 300 mile journey and if you don't run into any traffic you are going to be early. We had to be at the club for 6pm – it was only 4pm. Luckily I had told Steve, who was recuperating after his heart surgery at home, that if we had time we would call in to see him. There were only two kids on the street when we arrived at Steve's home, which was a council flat in the heart of Withywood, a large south Bristol council estate. They were probably on the way home from school. As we got out of the car to go into Steve's flat they casually glanced across

– not many stretch limos in Withywood. Their faces were a picture of amazement. I'd love to know what went through their minds. We spent about half an hour at Steve's and there was probably a group of about ten kids when we left. To make sure I was spot-on with the timings I had arranged for some refreshments to be available for Frank before we got to the club. As my parent's home was two minutes from the club and they were on holiday, it seemed a good idea to have the refreshments there. So Jayne (my wife-to-be) and my sister, Deb, had the pleasure of having tea with Frank. We got to the club on time at 6pm. Obviously, word had got out and there were people everywhere, as well as the members.

As we made our way into the club, the phone was thrust in my hand. "It's the TV," somebody said. "We understand Frank Bruno will be at the club tonight and we would like to do an interview," was the request. My response was quite short. "He is here now, you had your chance and blew it – no!" Both channels got the same answer. In reality, you can't stop the press from turning up but they were told to keep off the premises and they managed to get their interviews on the pavement outside the club when he left. The formal interview was done by a young black BBC Radio Bristol presenter Clive Myrie and he had Frank all to himself in the club's quiet room with just a couple of members present. The evening was wonderful and Frank was everything you would have expected him to be while in the public arena, absolutely brilliant. But away from the public, in the journey to the club he was different, very quiet, devoid of any meaningful conversation, almost lonely.

As well as celebrities, the role of guest of honour was sometimes offered to one of the club's family. Bert Abrahams, Roy James and Steve, himself, were bestowed with that honour, Steve immediately after his retirement.

11

Holidays

Our visits to Cornwall for our annual summer holidays had established a deep love of all things Cornish for many of the attendees, so much so that some members from that period established homes there. Chris Sherman discovered The Count House in Botallack, a folk club. Many of those on holiday with the club would take the opportunity to visit The Count House and by doing so established a great relationship with two of its favourite performers, Brenda Wootton and John the Fish. These were the heady days of the middle 60s; with Dylan at his best (some would say). Regular visitors to the Folk Club were artists like Ralph McTell, Michael Chapman and Alex Atterson. Brenda and John would join the older members and helpers (old enough to drink) for lunch during the holiday and it wasn't long before the duo would be performing their first concert outside their beloved Cornwall – at Bedminster Down Boys' Club on Friday 13 October 1967. When The Count House closed, Brenda opened The Pipers' Folk Club at St Buryan – and BDBC went with them. In 1970, Brenda and John were guests of honour at the club's Open Night, the ultimate tribute for the club's love of the first Lady of Cornwall. Songs like *Lamorna* and *Camborne Hill* would engage the mass voices of our BDBC Male Voice Choir, who would then sit in sheer awe of her singing *The White Rose* and *I'm Troubled*. I can only describe Brenda's voice as one of the most beautiful that I have had the privilege to have heard.

We normally kept away from the more popular attractions of St Ives and Land's End. Even visits to the town of Penzance were infrequent as the beauty of local beaches at Treen, Porthcurno, Sennen, and even Portheras Cove were preferred. We bought local produce from St Just and immersed ourselves within the community we stayed in. Early club holidays were based at Rosemergy Cottage, attached to a farm between Zennor and Morvah. When that closed, we moved to Carnyorth, just along the road from the historic Geevor Tin Mine. It was at Carnyorth that we witnessed the devastation of the Fastnet Yacht Race in August 1979, where eighteen people died over a three day period as a Force 11 gale hit the area.

Rosemergy's facilities were somewhat sparse. There were three bedrooms upstairs, two downstairs rooms that were used for staff bedrooms and a large kitchen/dining area. Most of the domestic issues were created due to the fact that there was only one toilet. When numbers going on the holidays increased, we installed a bell tent in the garden with two Elson toilets, separated with bits of sheeting. At the end of the holiday someone was tasked with digging a large hole to dispense with two weeks of human excrement – wonderful. It was during one holiday when the weather had been particularly bad that many of us had congregated in the general kitchen area chatting – the wind was howling outside. Suddenly the door opened and Bob Lewington (one of the voluntary staff on the holiday) walked in rather flustered. Now, Bob was a lovely bloke – he was in his early twenties and suffered from a hearing impediment, which meant his words were very pronounced to make his annunciation clear. He was also very religious. Anyway, Bob suddenly appeared and with very carefully pronounced words said, "The toilet tent's blown down". "Sorry Bob," someone said, "what did you say?" Bob was obviously exasperated and his voice raised a few decibels. "THE TOILET TENT HAS BLOWN DOWN." What had happened was that Bob was sat on one of the Elsons (which is simply a bucket with a lid on it), doing what comes naturally and a sudden gust of wind had brought the tent down on top of him. Bob had managed to scramble out and, utterly flustered, made it back inside the cottage. Now, Dave Phillips was in the group in the kitchen and Waffler, as we liked to call him, reacted first to the crisis. We all followed him outside and sure enough there was the tent on the floor – with the wind blowing like hell. Dave stood forward –"let's all grab a corner" he shouted and marched into the middle of the tent – just as another huge gust of wind picked the tent up, with the two Elsons, and slung it all in the air. The tent went in one direction –the two Elsons went straight up, flipped and came down depositing their contents everywhere.

Cornwall's weather could be unpredictable so activities on club holidays had to be varied to suit. As the membership changed over the years, so those running the holidays had to adapt the programme of activities. We ate healthily. Steve always recalled the first time he took the club away when, as they didn't have a vehicle, he took all the food with them. They lived on spam and beans for two weeks. Future holidays ensured that we had established contacts with fresh suppliers, butchers, bakers, etc. Before going out for the day, we would make and pack all the sandwiches or rolls, fruit and cake – and the food would be transported from the van to the beach. At lunchtime the members would sit and Longer would dish out the food. It must have been a wonderful sight for all the holidaymakers on the beach to see a group of twenty or so boys arrive and make camp adjacent to them. We would sing, we would play games, we would entertain the whole beach at times – much to the pleasure of some and the dismay of others. We were never bored. One afternoon with a little time on our hands we decided to entertain the passing motorists.

The roads in front of Rosemergy were very narrow, forcing vehicles to slow down to a virtual stop to pass. Phil 'Pippo' Stacey was always up for a laugh so we put together the follow-ing: suitably dressed in a top jacket, two of us would stop the

The club in Cornwall 1969

The clubs' adventure centre, Tal-y-sarn

Barry and Bratch on a skiing trip to Scotland

oncoming traffic. "Good afternoon" were our opening words to the driver. "Sorry to bother you but we come from the local asylum and one of our inmates has absconded. Would you have seen him?" With that, Phil would jump up from behind a nearby wall dressed in pyjamas and a bobble hat, scream-ing and shouting and making a hell of a noise. "There he is," someone would shout – and we would all run off in pursuit, leaving the motorists open-jawed. Unfortunately, on one occa-sion the motorist decided to help us and went screeching off down the road in pursuit of poor Phil.

After the first visit to Cornwall in 1965, the club travelled to their holiday retreat in the back of a furniture van, normally provided by Buglers, a local firm. There were no motorways so the journey could be tortuous. Steve's many stories about Cornwall holidays vividly capture the time when Harry, the driver, refused to stop due to the volume of traffic. So the members were forced to pee in crisp bags before (some of them) sending them high in the air onto the roofs of the cars travelling in the opposite direction. Then there was another occasion when Harry arrived at the club for the annual jaunt with two large carrier bags. "I've brought some reading material for the lads," he said to Steve. And before Steve had time to react, two bags full of pornographic (well soft porn in those days – Parade, etc) disappeared among our holidaymakers.

In the early holidays we had less and wanted less. We were happy and enjoyed each other's company – sometimes doing nothing more than chatting. Oddly enough we ate very well, there was no such thing as fast food, we ate properly cooked meals and we ate together. Of course, things were slightly regimented, they had to be. We were divided into three groups normally: cooking, cleaning and sandwiches – all hopefully self-explanatory. There was no alcohol. Yes, the staff would go for a meal with Brenda and John at some point but they didn't disappear to the pub every night. Any member that attended a Cornwall holiday during that period would have had a wonderful time and would have lasting memories. You didn't need any money as we didn't really go anywhere to buy anything.

But as time passed, club members wanted more and sometimes demanded more. Even some of the staff thought they were entitled to a night off to visit the pub. Nothing in life stays the same forever and my last Cornwall holidays as a member of the staff team will be remembered as being vastly different from the first ones I attended as a member. In the summer of 1986, with Steve having health problems, he asked me and Bratch to help with Cornwall. Bratch ran the first week, which was juniors, I would do the second week – seniors. Steve would come but he would limit himself to the cooking. The middle Saturday would be change-over day. Bratch returned with the juniors and we then re-loaded with the seniors for the journey back to Cornwall.

There were some people staying for both weeks. There were seniors who were staffing on the first week and attending as members on the second. And there were just a few staff who were supporting on both weeks. When we pulled up at Carnyorth, we were greeted by a senior member who had to be supported by a member of staff because he was pissed. I can smile about it all now but let's just say that I wasn't best pleased. I wouldn't say it was the most dynamic group of staff that could have been assembled and I had the other concern that one of the members of staff was a parent who had never done anything like this before. The consolation was that with Steve and Our Rog doing the cooking, at least we would be well-fed – which we were.

For me, it is important on holidays like this to keep everyone active. It's easy to lose everyone through boredom and very difficult to get them focused again. When the rain and mist didn't clear all day on the Sunday, I prayed that Monday would be better. It wasn't. We awoke Monday morning to the same thick Cornwall mist and rain. I needed to do something quick – so I got everyone together. "Put your shorts on, we are off to play football." They looked at me as if I had lost the plot. "But, Lou, it's raining and we can't see ten yards. (Yes, still 'yards' sixteen years after we went metric) in front of us." "I don't care, we are all going," was my reply. We all crammed in the van and went off to the local football pitch. It was pissing down with rain, you couldn't see anything really. We all got absolutely drenched. The van looked like it had been immersed in water when we got back – all shivering, freezing cold and laughing our heads off. I needed just one member of staff to be on-board with me (apart from the cooks) and that was Mike Palmer. Mike knew as much as I did what we needed to do and he was there alongside from the start. Running a holiday is very demanding. You feel that you owe it to everyone to ensure they have a good time – which is difficult.

Cornwall, while being possibly the club's favourite holiday destination between 1964 – 89, wasn't the only one. Although some of the more elaborate trips couldn't really be called holidays.

There were numerous trips to Kerne Bridge Adventure Centre until the club purchased its own adventure centre near Crickhowell. However, another early holiday destination wasn't too far from the club itself. The Whitsun Camp at Velvet Bottom was a great favourite for many members during the 60s and 70s. Velvet Bottom sits in a small valley just above Cheddar in the Mendip Hills, near the village of Charterhouse. There was no electricity or running water and certainly no modern toilets. This was good old-fashioned camping at its best. We would send out a small group out to the site on the Friday morning and they would erect all the tents. They would either be the old bell tents or a ridge tent (usually for the staff) – and then there would be the normal 'toilet tent', containing a couple of Elsons, and then a separate urinal area. The urinal area was a hand dug trench where you simply stood and peed. We would construct a kitchen area that would be equipped with trestle tables for eating.

We didn't do a lot. We created all our own entertainment. Football, touch rugby, volleyball and then there was Smithy's Hill. The ground would be best described as a trifle undulating. It wasn't in any shape or form flat! We got our water and milk from the local farmer and took most other things with us. Occupation of the tents was based around age group, apart from Miffer, who always slept in the staff tent – thankfully. There was only one minor issue that would sometimes crop up – adders!

Now, the adder is the only venomous snake native to the United Kingdom and the Mendips has its fair share of them – especially around Velvet Bottom. On one occasion, Paul Yo Yo Ewins decided to wake up a group of us in the early hours (early for us) with the now immortal words – "Is this an adder?" Having expressed our dismay at being disturbed with a number of choice expletives, the question was then asked, "What the

**** did you say?" Paul was a simple-minded soul "I was just wondering if this was an adder?" came the response. I have no idea what on earth made him do what he had done but, having got up for an early morning emptying of the bladder moment, he was ambling back to the tent and came across one of the biggest adders I have seen. He promptly picked it up by its tail, stuck it in a box and then decided to get a second opinion on what it was – by asking us! Needless to say, we didn't stay in the tent for long and Yo Yo ambled off to get one of the staff to detach the adder's head. They didn't and it was duly released a long way from the camp site. Appropriate footwear was an absolute must at Whitsun Camp.

These were the days before mobile phones, computers and all the rest of the personal entertainment technology that we currently have. We created our own entertainment. In the evenings we would gather around a fire, we would chat, tell jokes, make toast and, of course, sing. Many of the songs were traditional that would have been heard around Scout campfires but they would all be accompanied with actions. *The Music Man* was an absolute must and would guarantee the evening would get off to a good start. The other tradition was the relaying of ghost stories – or tales of the unexpected. This was always good for a laugh, especially if there were younger members in attendance. Many of the stories had elements of truth, some were just pure fiction – unfortunately it wasn't always possible to tell the difference. *The ghost of Velvet Bottom* was always good to set the nerves tingling and would nearly always be accompanied by a scream from the darkness at the crucial point in the story. Of course, there have been those that attended these camps who have heard the screams of the Lady Charlotte as she walked down the gravel path at the side of our camp in the middle of the night!

Many of the Cornish songs that adorned Show Down over the years were heralded at Whitsun Camp. *Camborne Hill, Dark as a Dungeon, Fly Away, Henry my son* and of course the brilliant *I Had Some Chickens*. There was of course no alcohol involved – there were no inhibitions either – we were all just happy to share each other's company and enjoy ourselves. The only downside of these trips was if you were chosen to empty the Elson toilets at the end of the camp, which involved the digging of a large hole and the subsequent emptying of the contents!

Kerne Bridge is situated in Herefordshire, about 3.5 miles south of Ross-on-Wye. The centre was in two parts. The old railway station provided the main room, toilets, some bedrooms and a kitchen while outside a converted train carriage provided accommodation for about twelve.

The seniors had used the facilities on a couple of occasions before Steve decided to take the juniors there in 1969. I had just returned from the senior holiday in Cornwall and was asked if I would go along to help out. A few lads from the Withywood group I had been working with on junior nights were attending the holiday. The age for joining juniors was eleven, so quite how Nicky Johns' brother managed to get on the holiday at barely ten years old I still haven't worked out but attend he did. The staff group was Steve, Esky and myself. Dave Phillips, who was the junior leader, joined us during the week. It was my first experience of staffing a club holiday. I suppose the memorable thing about that holiday, apart from having a great time, was the development of my relationship with that group from Withywood. Some years later, I returned to Kerne Bridge with a group of juniors – it was the first holiday I had ever run as junior leader. I had discussed the proposal with Steve many months earlier and he was absolutely supportive. The members that came (all juniors) were largely made up of the notorious Headley Park Mob. I should have twigged something was up when they all put their names down early on to attend. I think the parents had got together and decided they could collectively have a week's peace. I was blessed with

the support of Jean and Don Smith that week. They were the parents of Rob Smith, who was a senior member and a young junior club helper. Jean and Don did all the cooking – they were brilliant. You can't really get lost at Kerne Bridge as the area was quite restricted. However, within an hour of us arriving some of the party had found what they thought was an apple tree and devoured much of the fruit. I was blissfully unaware of this until about 2am in the morning when some of them started throwing up everywhere. Having sorted that out over the first few days, I then had a problem with one individual who was continually complaining of bad stomach pains. I won't reveal his name but if he ever reads this he'll know who I am talking about. As my concerns grew and I was thinking of taking him to a local doctor, one of his mates looked up and said, "Well, he has only just come out of hospital." So keen were his parents to get rid of him for a week, they forgot to mention that he had been in hospital for a few days before we left. I drove him back to Bristol that night, deposited him back with his mother and, for once (following Don's wise counsel), kept my mouth shut.

In 1976, the club organised a safari to Morocco. The brainwave of Brian Howarth it was originally planned to run along the same lines as the London Union of Youth Clubs' Expedition of 1974. The planning of this project involved twelve months of research. The aims were identified and recorded:

To enable youngsters to live together under difficult and stressful situations.

To widen their experience and knowledge of differing cultures and societies.

To equip them with experience to enable them to plan and execute such adventurous activities for themselves.

To develop potential qualities of leadership.

To enable them to extend their own level of endurance and fitness.

They departed the club on Tuesday 10 August 1976 and arrived at their destination on the Saturday, four days later. Fifteen members and four staff went on the three week trip. Their thoughts and memories are documented in the club's archives. There were holidays in Switzerland, the United States and Scotland. There were two trips to Nepal. They were small groups but they provided unique opportunities for members to have life-changing experiences. This type of holiday needed the drive and enthusiasm of individuals to deliver them and there was always somebody willing to do it.

A decision taken at the club's parliament on the 31 October 1977 was to have a far-reaching impact on the club's residential work for years to come. That decision was to research and purchase its own adventure centre.

The acquirement of Tal-y-sarn can largely be attributed to Bob Plumb, a retired Rolls Royce Engineer who had walked into the club so many years earlier and who had virtually single-handedly raised the money for the club's own adventure centre. Bob was not typical of the voluntary staff that the club had at that time. In fact, in many ways you could say he looked out-of-sorts in the often loud, bustling environment of a packed youth organisation. However, he had this wonderful ability to capture the attention of the membership, especially those who would join them in this unique project. Following the initial purchase of the property, which is situated on the edge of the Brecon Beacon National Park, approximately seven miles southwest of Abergavenny, Bob would organise work parties to undertake the remedial work that was required. In the years that followed, hundreds of young people benefited from the legacy that Bob Plumb provided.

12

New Leader

It's difficult, some forty years on, to put into context the relationship between the staff and the membership at that time, compared to the harsh reality of the world we live in now. Many parents were involved with the club. They would regularly welcome members of staff to their houses for social occasions and there would, therefore, be some social contact with some of the members outside of normal club activities. There would be some idolisation of some of the staff who were good at this sport or that sport, by certain members – or of those who could play a musical instrument or sing. As they grew through the club into adulthood, some members continued with these friendships, usually through a mutual interest in an activity, like volleyball or canoeing. The Withywood group of 1969 consisted originally of four lads – Nicky Johns, Kevin Joxson, Chris Messenger and Mark Spear, who was the oldest. Bedminster Down was still pretty territorial in those days. In fact, both Hartcliffe Boys' Club and Withywood Youth Club were closer to where the group lived than BDBC. However, such was the reputation of the club growing, this group decided to try us out. For two of them, their love of the club continued until its closure. Mark Spear's parents became helpers in their own right. Beryl became a member of the ladies' group, and Brian actually went on to run a successful club football team. Nicky Johns went on to become a professional footballer. He returned to the club as an Open Night guest of honour in 1984 and was a loyal supporter up until its closure. There was a unique relationship between every faction of the club community and a universal acceptance of what was right. Over the following years there was a fundamental change in society. One of those, most significant for us at BDBC, was that many parents became less interested in what their children were doing. Giving children their time was replaced with giving children their money. Fewer parents got involved with the club, many of them were completely disinterested – even going so far as to moan quite vociferously when the club was shut for any reason. The knock-on effect was that a resource pool for voluntary staff dried up and we often lapsed from one staffing crisis into another.

Staffing was a continuous problem through many of club's years after the initial heydays of the 60s and early 70s. As previously stated, the club's attempts to find a suitable permanent assistant leader following the resignation of Brian Howarth in 1978 was largely unsuccessful. There were appointments made but none of them reached the expectation at that time – and I'm certain that Steve wasn't the easiest person to work with. In agreement with the funders (Bristol City Council), the salary for the assistant leader's post was converted into part-time paid sessions. This was a new phenomenon for the club and one that many people were not comfortable with. The club had its strength in our voluntary helper support – the concept that some of these volunteers would now be paid and others wouldn't, could create problems. I accept the principle that if people were going to commit themselves to attending the club two/three sessions a week, and were undertaking quality youth work, then there wouldn't be a problem. The issue would always be whether the club was getting value for money? Over the years, there were some excellent practitioners in those positions that had come through the club as members and, yes, there were others that probably weren't as effective. Two of the best were Barry Lovell and Steve

Bratchel – they came through the transition of the change of club leader, and remained absolutely resolute to their own convictions throughout. They both resigned when the time was right for them due to those convictions and then both came back to support me at the turbulent end of the club's life.

The frailties of this change were never more apparent to me then when picking up the gauntlet when Steve went off sick. Suddenly, I was faced with claims for sessions that I wasn't comfortable with – such as driving the club van to football matches. When I challenged Steve about this practice he confessed that he didn't know that was the case – he had assumed much. Whether these payments were right or wrong will always be subjective – it's about value for money. For me this didn't amount to a good use of the club's finances, so after consultation with the club's treasurer I stopped it – but the football teams still got to their matches. There will be those who read this who will point out that I became a paid member of staff – and they would be correct. I was asked to by Steve on the basis that he needed someone 'paid to run the club' in his absence – the accountability was huge and I accepted the role on that basis. That position changed on the appointment of Steve's replacement.

The appointment of Russ Cooper as Steve's successor in August 1990 was to change the club forever.

Steve had announced his retirement on the grounds of ill health and the management committee had begun the process of finding a replacement. Key to that process was the involvement of the membership. The membership had been critical of the club's management committee following the failure of the previous assistant leader's post – they hadn't been involved and knew the individuals weren't right for the club. The club's chairman at this time was David Baker and he was adamant the appointment of any new leader had to have the 100 percent endorsement of the membership. This was fine by me and a majority of the rest of the management committee. It didn't have the support, it would seem, of the external representatives on the management committee. Trevor Jones was the general secretary of the Avon & Bristol Federation and he had reservations. Why he had reservations was unclear to me. However, a letter was received by David Baker from the chairman of the Federation expressing their concerns. The letter was read by a few people but David, his normal tactful self, returned the letter unopened and nothing more was said.

I was still heading up the leadership team and the obvious question was asked – am I going to apply for the job? One of the people who asked me that very question was Trevor Jones, who quickly followed it with the statement, "You won't get it if you do, as you're not qualified." I quickly reminded Trevor that the management committee could appoint who they wanted – the relevance to me being qualified or not would only affect Bristol City Council's decision on whether to fund the position or not. As it was, I had no intention of applying for the role. I had returned to Bristol Water following ten years of being self-employed and I had a young family to cater for. The long hours and low pay of a youth worker was no attraction, no matter how rewarding. That was just as well, as Trevor clearly had someone in mind for the post – his name was, Russell Cooper.

We interviewed two people for the post, Russ and one other. The formal interviews followed a very demanding selection process where both candidates attended the club and spent the night with the membership. Two members sat on the formal interview panel along with representatives from the Avon Federation and Bristol City Council. Russ' CV was clearly very good and he had considerable experience. The other candidate was inexperienced. There was one problem. The membership had decided that they wanted the inexperienced candidate – not Russ Cooper. Russ had come over as very confident at the interview, bordering arrogance – the members didn't like it.

David Baker was without doubt, without any disrespect to any of the others, the finest chairman the club ever had. He was certainly the only one who had a long-term successful relationship with Steve – they had the utmost respect for one another. David tasked me with taking the members involved with the interview away from the club's quiet room (where the interviews were being held) to somewhere seemingly less oppressive to chat about their thoughts. There were a number of members hanging around – those that had been involved in the pre-interview nights. We sat and we chatted. The key thing I told them was to have somebody that could build on the club's success following Steve. The club was nationally acclaimed, it was at the forefront of all groundbreaking youth work – was it wise to put somebody in a position that had little experience, even if he did seem like a very nice guy? And so Russ Cooper was appointed and, for the record, the other candidate was appointed later at another club in the city – however, he didn't last long.

To put it into context, Russ Cooper taking over from Steve Long is like the modern day David Moyes replacing Sir Alex Ferguson. There were going to be changes, whichever way you looked at it, and change can sometimes be painful. But at least Trevor Jones was happy; he had got the appointment he wanted. His relationship with Russ went back to a time at King Alfred Boys' Club in Hampshire – when Trevor was leader and Russ a senior member who then went on to become the club leader. He went from there to the Downside Club in London, prior to joining us at BDBC.

Looking back so many years on, it is obvious that the club needed to change. Regrettably so many of us got wrapped up in its success we failed to notice how things were changing around us. However, the immediate changes were brought about by the new leader. I continued with my role on the management committee for around eighteen months following Russ' appointment and then stood down. I made a promise that I would continue to support the club and stay in contact – which I did.

The official retirement dinner for Steve took place at the club in May 1990 and was attended by many of the people that he had known and worked with during his time at the club. Representatives came from the National Association of Boys' Clubs in London and there were many local dignitaries. Steve was presented with a word processor. Writing was his passion, along with singing, and that was how he would spend his retirement. He paid one last visit to the club in July, just two months later when he was the guest of honour for the club's Open Night.

Steve with Dave Scarborough

Steve died on the 1 December 1991, some fifteen months after his official retirement. His dream of retiring, writing and continuing his singing was short-lived. It was always going to be a challenge. I'm sure all of us who knew him well realised that. However, he was in a positive mindset when he left the club. He was in a new relationship and had lots to look forward to. Regrettably, the relationship broke down and Steve spiralled into a deeper and deeper depression. When you devote the whole of your life to something as Steve did, the reality of living without it was hard. When I was running the club in his absence, he would often say how proud he was that it was his people, his staff, that were keeping the club going – and this was proof of everything that was good about BDBC. And then he would look at me and say, "The trouble is, Lou, there is also something sad for me that the club has gone on without me – it doesn't need me." It was far from the truth – we only set out to hold the fort, based on the foundations that he had laid. There was no going back when he retired and when the relationship he was in failed, he had nothing.

Steve's time in hospital prior to his death was difficult and personally very painful. Initially he didn't want any visitors other than David Baker, his mum and me. Many people wanted to visit him and I had to tell them no – even my own father. The comments that were made of me in some cases were not pleasant – I appeared to be the victim of some people's frustration.

Hundreds of mourners packed St Oswald's Church, just fifty metres from the club, for his funeral. They represented all parts of the community, all areas of youth work, from education and politics, from the world of theatre and most importantly they represented twenty-five years of Boys' Club membership. It would be impossible for me to put into words the impact this man had on the lives of so many young people. Steve's legacy would live on through the generations of people whose lives he had influenced. I have often been asked, "Why wasn't Steve honoured, why didn't he get an MBE for instance?" Well, there is a story behind that. Just before Steve died I was with his mum at his flat, Claypiece Heights, as it was affectionately known. "You know, Andy," she said "they wanted Steve to have a medal but he turned it down." I nodded agreement but had no idea what she was talking about. Following his death I found this in the personal possessions he left me.

1O DOWNING STREET

LONDON SW1A 2AA

From the Principal Private Secretary

IN CONFIDENCE   26 November 1986

Sir,

    I have the honour to inform you that The Queen has been graciously pleased to approve the Prime Minister's recommendation that the British Empire Medal (B.E.M.) be awarded to you.

    This award is due to be announced in the New Year Honours List to be published on 31 December 1986; this letter must be treated as strictly confidential until then.

    The award will be presented to you locally by the Lord-Lieutenant of your county or by a Minister of the Crown as The Queen's representative. Details of the time and place of the presentation will be sent to you in due course.

    I should be glad if you would kindly complete the enclosed form and send it to me by return of post.

                    I am, Sir,
                    Your obedient Servant,

                    N.L.Wicks

S T Long Esq
8 Claypiece Road
Withywood
Bristol
BS13 9DP

Also in his possessions was the acknowledgment of Steve's reply declining the award.

Over the next few years, Russ embarked on changing the face of the club – however, parliament remained. I have discussed at length with many former club colleagues how those changes evolved and why. Whether it was a conscious decision on his part I don't know but Russ seemed to have a desire to alienate himself from many of the existing staff, especially the ladies' group. He was more comfortable with developing his relationship with the more senior members, quickly forming an inner sanctum. He clashed hard with some of the existing staff and some of them left.

During one of my lunchtime visits to the club during that period, Russ stated that he had received an anonymous letter through the post. I can't remember now whether it had been hand delivered or posted. Anyway, the letter questioned the fact that members had been staying overnight at his home in Headley Park. "But why would they?" I asked him. His response was typical Russ. "Why not? I'm not doing anything wrong." And that answer summed up one of Russ' failings. It didn't matter what anyone else thought – supremely confident or arrogant beyond belief? That one conversation would come back to haunt me many years later. I told Russ that he should take the letter to the police, which he did – and I had the pleasure of having my fingerprints taken to eliminate me from their enquiries as I had handled the letter.

Russ developed a very strong senior membership team. There is no doubt he had the ability to relate to many of the members and became a major influence on some of their lives in a positive way. The introduction of summer camps for children in the community was a major success and enhanced the club's revenue. They were staffed by senior members who had gone through a strict training regime. Like Steve, he was demanding in his levels of expectation.

The club's successful drama period came to an end but

the Christmas shows continued – they became more pantomime-themed. Again, not a criticism, but a reflection on the differing strengths of the leaders. I had the pleasure of witnessing both our sons perform in Christmas shows at the club. Ben appeared as Tiny Tim in a version of Charles Dickens' *A Christmas Carol* and while Sam appeared in a number of shows, his performance as Dorothy in a version of *The Wizard of Oz* was the probable highlight (for us, not for him). I am not sure if anyone else can claim to have had three generations of their family in club shows.

13

Fundraising

There were two issues that plagued both the full-time leaders throughout their tenures at different times and to different degrees – voluntary staff and funding. It was to a rallying call for funding that I responded in 1999. If you're involved in any voluntary organisation to any degree, there will always be occasions when you have to get off your ass and do something.

Throughout my time at the club, I endeavoured always to do my bit with fundraising. Sponsored walks, sponsored swims and selling raffle tickets – we would all muck in as members. I remember taking part in my first sponsored walk in 1967 (I think). It was over the Mendip Hills to Wells and back to Winford. Only one person completed it and that was Jim Marriot. In the school summer holidays, we would gather at The Horsefair in Bristol selling raffle tickets to all who passed. This was NABC's national raffle and the club got a percentage of the takings. The only problem was that you had to ask all prospective buyers the same question. "How many people will attend football league matches on November the such-and-such?" If ever a question was going to put somebody off buying a ticket that was it. If we had sold enough tickets we would be given some money to get some chips from the chip shop at the bottom of Christmas Steps. One year, we had a sponsored penalty shoot-out at the home of Bristol City Football Club – with their goalkeeper, Ray Cashley, between the posts. We all had to take five penalties and I was sponsored to the tune of £20 per penalty – a fair bit of money in those days. "Who is on £20 a penalty?" Ray asked one of the members taking part. They pointed to me. I will always maintain that four out of five penalties against a First Division keeper isn't bad – and it was my ability to deceive the goalkeeper that resulted in him going the opposite way to the ball for the first four. Others have a somewhat different opinion!

The cornerstone of the club's fundraising was Club Week. For years we pre-delivered envelopes to the local community, normally with a covering letter about the club. Then a week later, we would go out and collect them back again. Regrettably, it was always winter time when we were undertaking this challenge and often raining. It was organised like a military operation – every person knew exactly what street they should be collecting in and sometimes the numbers of the houses. The plan was originally put together by Dave Phillips and then carried on by Dave Scarborough. The club would close on the nights we were collecting the money. The members were tasked with bringing the envelopes back and then counting the contents and that of the tins. Great cries of joy would be heard if the amount collected was greater than the previous year's – yes, we kept a record of every amount from every area! I remember the night we first hit a £1,000 on the first night of collecting – the fact that the local community gave us that degree of support was wonderful. Yes, there were odd moments when there were issues and that left a nasty taste at the time, but they were minimal. There was always competition between us and Hartcliffe Boys' Club, so any attempt by their members to collect on our patch caused outrage. The same issue used to arise when we were selling tickets down at The Horsefair. Ernest Curtis, the leader of Hartcliffe and affectionately known as Ernie, would always be on-site at the same time. There would be rows over who had the best pitches for selling and rumours that Ernie paid his members a bonus if they sold a certain amount – we just got fish and chips!

We would often advertise Club Week with some bizarre publicity stunt in the first years, like touring the streets on the back of a lorry or a relay team running around the area with lit torches. Another money-making scheme came as a consequence of the traffic chaos on the A38 during the summer, as holidaymakers made their way painstakingly down the A roads (prior to the M5) to Devon and Cornwall. The A38 would come to a standstill, engines would overheat, there was a lack of amenities on the route and an opportunity was presented. So between 1971 and 1973 we ran a summer cafe on consecutive Saturdays, from 4am until 4pm. Holidaymakers would be encouraged by a few locally positioned handmade signs. Our neighbours, the Ex-Servicemen's Club, gave us permission to use their car park and holidaymakers would pour off the busy road to get something to eat and drink and use the toilets.

What would have been really beneficial back then would have been one of those 'no win, no fee' insurance companies. I can picture it very clearly still. Two solid queues of traffic virtually stationary coming out and going in to Bristol on the A38. The Cross Hands pub at one end and the King's Head pub at the other. Suddenly a passenger yelled, "Oh, look at that Bridge", as Brunel's spectacular construction came into view – everyone looked to their left including the driver, the car in front stopped and our holidaymakers drove up the back of the car in front of them. Every Saturday during the summer this would be witnessed – great viewing.

Anyway, the cafe was a one off and great fun. Parents, helpers and members all pitched in – some operating in shifts, others stayed all day. Most of the members spent their time waiting on tables. We had a fixed menu – sandwiches, beans/egg/cheese on toast, salads etc – nothing fancy but well-cooked and presented. There was no dishwasher so everything was washed up by hand. They were heady days with the likes of Colin Jones at his flamboyant best and Gran Towels making her legendry salads. Husband and wife teams, the parents of members, spent virtually every Saturday helping Jean and Don Smith, Brian and Beryl Spear and, of course, our own Dave and Di. Yes, it was hard work but we had a laugh along the way – and, of course, there is the legend of Barry Moretoast. We didn't have many non-white members at that time, Leonard Scotland was probably the only one when this tall gangling black teenager turned up one Saturday to join the club. We were slightly taken aback. Now, the story goes that Steve explained to him that the club was actually shut for the summer but if he would like to help out at the cafe he was welcome to, then he could join when the club reopened in September. His name was Barry. Barry seemed enthusiastic and was welcomed into the fold. Barry was put on the toaster – egg on toast, cheese on toast, etc. When more toast was needed Barry would respond, normally to the request, "Barry, more toast?". And so the legend of Barry Moretoast was born – we never found out his real surname and he never returned to the club after that summer.

We raised well over a £1,000 with the summer cafe – and it provided a huge contribution to the club's first extension. Enterprise at its best.

Sponsored events happened regularly – swims, walks, runs and a whole range of various events.

In 1978, I ran from Bristol to Weston with my good friend, Tim Fowler. I worked with Tim at the time and he rallied to support me when I talked about the idea. Our support driver on that day was Barry Lovell. This was the first of the four major fundraisers I did during my time at the club and Barry was alongside me as my support on every occasion. For the two cycle rides I can safely say that Barry was solely responsible for me completing them – especially the second one.

For the record, the second one was a walk from the club to its adventure centre in South Wales. We started on Good Friday, 17 April 1981. Dave Jones was going to walk the whole journey with me, with a number of members supporting over the two days. They were Dave Bennett, Mike Burton, Darren Sheen, Darren Jones and Paul McCarthy. Dave's parents, Colin and Shirley, had been helpers at the club when they tragically lost their lives, along with Dave's brother, Andrew, in the Basle Air Disaster. The tragedy hit the whole community hard but for Dave the loss was immense. Eight years on, he joined me for this sponsored walk, just six weeks after having knee surgery. Dave managed to keep going for twenty-six miles before having to retire. It was a huge effort on his part. We walked for twelve hours that day and covered the first 33.3 miles. The rest of the walk we completed on the Sunday, just over another twelve miles – my notes say never again – didn't keep that promise, did I?

Number three was a cycle ride from the adventure centre to the club and the fourth (and last) was a cycle ride from London to the club.

The funeral of Colin, Shirley and Andrew Jones was at my local church, the Zion Methodist on Bishopsworth Road. It was the first funeral I had ever attended. Regrettably, over the coming years I would attend many more.

There is nothing worse than having to stand shoulder-to-shoulder with club colleagues at the funeral of one of our members or indeed friends. Logic says that if you spend many years with any organisation you will, no doubt, suffer such a loss at some time. Working with young people is different. No parent should have to suffer the loss of a child at such a young age. However many members we lost under these circumstances, it was too many.

There appeared to be a lack of adult support during Russ' time. Only he can answer to the question why. For me it was purely a call to arms – the club that I loved needed my support.

Russ had seemingly replaced most of the adults with senior members. A few adults retained their commitment like Mike Palmer and Barry. There was quality in that senior members' team and these were undoubtedly the product of Russ' development strategy. Once again, I found myself back involved at the club on a voluntary basis. Most of the familiar names of the previous years had disappeared and had been replaced with the likes of Shaun Gould, Alex Ball, Pickle, Monksy and Mike Trought to name but a few. It was important for me to engage with these new young staff. Years later, some of these would turn out to be absolute rocks.

The battle for funding became even worse. What made the situation worse was the decision by Young Bristol (YB), the organisation we were affiliated to (originally the Bristol Federation of Boys' Clubs), to align themselves with the council's approach to funding, which was alienating any single sexed youth organisation. These battles had started during Steve's reign – so it wasn't a new issue. However, those umbrella organisations that were supposed to support their clubs had changed tack. The old stalwarts like Jack Clarke and Chris Willcox, both staunch Boys' Club people, had gone – replaced with individuals who were more intent on surviving themselves rather than standing up for the rights of the clubs they were supposed to be representing. It would ultimately lead to the closure of BDBC.

The other major problem facing the club at this time was the state of the building. There were major subsidence issues – the major cause being the fact that the club was built on an old tip. There were significant cracks in the original rear wall of the building and the gym floor was sinking. In 1999, we engaged a structural engineer to undertake a full report. His findings were of no surprise – the club needed to be rebuilt. One of the options we considered was to build elsewhere and several sites were looked at – alongside the football pitch on Bridgwater Road and a green field just past the King's Head public house were both ruled out after talks with the council. One option, however, did seem to have a better chance of progress. The sports field attached to the local junior school did have a dead corner that had possibilities. Russ and I would put together a very professional presentation and go along to one of the school's governing body meetings. Already on the school premises was a local Adventure Scout Group that operated from a small timber-built building. Our proposal was to build a brand new club for the young people of Bedminster Down. It would accommodate the Scout group, it would accommodate girls and, importantly, the facilities could be used by the school during the day.

I have to say that I thought our presentation was good, it was certainly professional. What we hadn't anticipated was the strength of the existing relationship between the school and the Scouts. Our plan was to build a £1m building that met the needs of all young people in the area. The school turned us down and gave the Scouts permission to build a new Scout hut. It was a decision that still amazes me today. Having said that, the Scouts have gone from strength to strength and provide a fantastic service to the community. The Scout leader was Alan Burnett, a school governor. I have to say that Alan wasn't my cup of tea, probably because we were involved in different areas of youth work. However, it again shows how the success of many youth organisations can largely be attributed to the dedication and professionalism of those running them. Tragically Alan died in a ballooning accident in 2011 but Blenheim Scouts still thrive on the platform he built.

In June 2002, I completed my final fundraising event. It was to be the most challenging. Having previously cycled the fifty-odd miles from the club's adventure centre in South Wales three years earlier, the idea of doing a ride from London to Bristol didn't seem too daunting – about 100 miles isn't it? The first cycle ride had been undertaken with Chris Densley and Tom Windows. Chris was a good friend and his wife, Ang, helped at junior club. They had three sons who attended club. Tom was one of the older senior members. Barry cycled alongside me and the support team was Russ and Mike Palmer.

The London ride was months in the planning and included many training days. I approached the same team. Chris agreed straight away but Tom was committed by work. We pulled in three others to do the ride – Nicky Jones, Alex Ball and Ben Hayes. Nick was a former member and had been part of the Headley Park Mob that occupied much of my time as junior leader many years previously. Alex had grown through the club and was now a member of the voluntary staff team. He was a young professional at Bristol City Football Club. Ben was a senior member and his inclusion was somewhat controversial. I wasn't comfortable with having a member participating. Neither Chris nor Nick had worked at the club as adult helpers. Additionally Ben was one of the more extrovert members, always had plenty to say and could sometimes cross those boundaries of acceptable behaviour. As it turned out, there were no issues – Ben was a credit to the club. We cycled over three days in June, the second day being the worst day of my life, as I cycled for ten hours in the rain and cold. At times the clouds and the road merged into one grey mass. I couldn't tell whether I was looking up or down. The others stopped along the route to watch England play the Argentine in the 2002 World Cup match. I declined that offer and cycled on. When I reached the end of the ride for the day I fell off the bike – physically and mentally exhausted. I owe the fact that I completed that day's ride and the whole journey to my good friend, Barry Lovell.

If that event hadn't pushed me to the absolute limits of endurance then what was going to happen next would surely do so.

It wasn't long before Bristol City Council delivered their fatal blow. There would be no more funding from September 2003. The council was focusing its support into

London to Bristol cycle ride

Neighbourhood Renewal Areas (NRAs). These were areas where deprivation indicators are considered to be the worst and therefore the areas of most need. The long battle with the authorities appeared to be coming to an end. What the council was offering was a sum of £12k to a locality youth project which must use the money to deliver mixed, new work only. We had been receiving a grant of £29k per annum. The local girls' club, which was being run by Goretta Thorne, the club's former secretary and member of voluntary staff, had applied for the grant. They would, however, have to change their constitution to do so.

It looked destined to be a classic case of us versus them, with the them being the girls' club. We considered applying for the grant and doing two mixed sessions per week. "We will not look favourably on that while you continue to do boys' only work," was the feedback from the council.

In July 2003, the situation was discussed at the club's

parliament. Ninety-four percent of the members said they would rather see the club close than accept the £12k and go part-time and mixed. We could probably survive for a few more years by selling the adventure centre and using the funds to finance the club. However, later developments would change that. After the summer break, the club reopened in September knowing this could be our final year – in October we issued a statement to that effect.

As Mondays go, it wasn't anything special at Bristol Water, a typical November day. I had a planned disciplinary hearing with an employee late in the afternoon and it was during a break from that that I got the message from one of the admin staff who worked in the section. "Andy, can you ring the police at the club?" We hadn't had many break-ins all the time the club had been opened but I naturally assumed it was something along those lines, though why they would ring me and not Russ, I was unsure. Anyway, during the break from those work activities I did just that. The club's phone was answered by somebody who identified himself as a policeman. I wasn't duly alarmed as if the club had been broken into or vandalised, they could well be inside the club. However, the policeman offered me no reason for them being inside the club, just a request to attend the premises immediately. Luckily, the disciplinary case had been adjourned and so I made my way to the club's premises, which was less than a minute's drive from work.

Some ten years later, the pain of what happened next is still very evident in the lives of many of us. I was met at the club by a plain clothes policeman, in fact, there were about four officers there all in plain clothes. I duly identified myself and was taken in to the leader's office. The officer spoke calmly and quietly. "Russ Cooper, the full-time leader of this club, has been arrested at his home this morning and is helping police with their enquiries regarding allegations of sexual offences involving young boys. The allegations are historic and do not relate to his time at Bedminster Down Boys' Club." I went quiet. I actually didn't know what to say. They then told me that they had contacted Mike Wells, who was the club's chairman at that time, and he advised them that it was probably best to talk to me – hence the phone call.

These officers were from a special unit in Bristol and they had attended Russ' home with officers from Hampshire that morning. I sat and talked with the police for around an hour. They would want to interview me again later and they would be in touch. They had collected up all the club's computers and taken away all the computer discs they could find. Everything had been labelled and put in large plastic bags and was being loaded into the back of a car outside. They couldn't expand on anything else but then asked me what my intentions were. In these situations there is no alternative – it didn't really matter whether the allegations were true or not. The interests of the members had to come first and therefore Russ would have to be suspended immediately. Russ had no keys to the club as they had been taken from him at his arrest and at that time he was still being interviewed at a police station in Lockleaze.

The Police left and I sat in the foyer pondering, What was going to happen next? I immediately phoned Jayne (the wife), briefly explained what had happened and then contacted Mike Wells and Dave Scarborough.

I opened the club that night and had the job of issuing a short statement later that evening to the staff and members alike. Russ was on leave of absence for the time being. Later that week, a more formal statement was issued explaining the allegations, which related to his time at King Alfred Boys' Club and that we would do our absolute best to maintain our service to the young people of Bedminster Down. Late that Monday night, I received a message from Russ that he had been released on bail and was now at home – and so I went to visit. Russ wouldn't or couldn't say much at all. I informed him that he had been suspended until further notice. He was not to go anywhere near the club or to make contact with any of the members. He understood the reasons fully. Later that week, I visited him again and managed to get the following: "That there was a degree of truth in some of the allegations." I didn't even know what the allegations were at that stage.

Needless to say, I was interviewed fully twice by the police, once at Lockleaze Police Station and once at home. I agreed to fully cooperate with their investigations and was asked to go on a fishing trip. This didn't involve rods and bait but it did involve talking discreetly to several current club members, who were identified as being at risk. This process went on for weeks – it was painful and depressing but had to be done. I knew all the individuals concerned. The reasons for the fishing trip was that some sexual predators groom their victims over many years. The police had mapped the route of the allegations of what happened at King Alfred and were looking for similarities at Bedminster Down.

Neither I nor the police found any evidence that any member of the club had been a victim of abuse. Russ remained on full-pay (there was no legal basis for not paying him) and pleaded his innocence until he appeared at Winchester Crown Court in November 2004, some twelve months later. He then admitted to five cases of indecent assault and three of gross indecency against boys. He was sentenced to two and a half years in prison. By that time the club had closed and to cap it all we had to pay him redundancy money!! Years later, there is still no evidence that anything untoward happened at the club during Russ' leadership. For a considerable time after, I was plagued with guilt. What if something had happened? It was part of my job to protect these kids, that's what management committees do; it's what governing bodies in schools do. If we can't protect them, who will? It's common knowledge that it often takes years for victims to come to terms with their abuse. Could any of us be sure about anything? I am not ashamed to say that the closure of the club, along with some of the circumstances surrounding it, caused me problems. It led to a month off work. Luckily, with the support of my family and friends and some professional help, I came out the other side. The harsh reality of what happened hasn't changed, but my ability to manage it has.

There will always be those people who are quick to judge those adults who get involved in working with young people, especially youth organisations. Whether it's sports teams, youth clubs or uniformed organisations, individuals have been subject to the innuendo, the strange looks, etc. The processes for eliminating the risks to those young people have improved, although vigilance will always be required. Luckily there were very few occasions at BDBC when we had cause to question the motives of any of the staff but they did happen. Prior to my joining in 1966, an adult helper had apparently been asked to leave, although there is nobody around now to expand on that. On the junior holiday to Lyme Regis in 1976, one of the senior members who was assisting me brought my attention to the behaviour of an adult, who was under consideration to replace me as junior leader when I finished at the end of that summer. Like a pair of very inefficient detectives we followed the adult one day and found him walking hand-in-hand along the beach with one of the junior members. When we returned to Bristol I sat down with Steve and went through everything. Steve confronted the individual and he left, maintaining his innocence. The saddest thing of all is that when I entered youth work as an adult in 1971, the priority was always the protection of the young people we worked with – in the final years the priority was self-protection – how depressing.

14

The Final Days

The Russ issue put a huge cloud over the club for the remaining time it stayed open. We appeared to be battling on all fronts – with the council for removing the funding, with Young Bristol, who were intent on being hostile towards us, and with our integrity as the rumours about Russ quickly circulated. Once again, I found myself at the helm of the club that I loved and had been such a huge part of my life. In true Bedminster Down style, we re-grouped as a voluntary staff team. There was no money to pay anyone so nobody was paid (apart from Russ Cooper!). We had to reduce the nights we could open – it wasn't physically possible to sustain five nights a week and weekend activities. There were virtually no adult helpers – Barry and Mike had already resigned, disillusioned with the way the club was going. Both of them had been helpers for many years and their loss was significant. Barry, in particular, had found it difficult to adapt to a change in the values of young people. They were no longer interested in such things as parliament or self-governance. They didn't want responsibility – they only wanted what they wanted – nothing else. I had a small team of young adult helpers – Shaun, Pickle, Alex, Monksy. Bratch and Barry immediately bounced back to help whenever they could – it was going to be tough until the end.

We hit the press with a number of briefings – the boys versus girls debate re-surfaced. The City Council attacked back – the local councillor promised support which didn't materialise. There were dramatic articles written in the press. Old press cuttings, newsreel and out-takes were unearthed and re-shown on the box. Young Bristol, the organisation that once supported the clubs that affiliated to it and shown loyalty to them for many years, did jack shit. Actually, I need to correct that, they did do something – they actually conspired to work against us, appearing to share an alliance with the girls' club to actually move into our premises when we vacated.

If we were to close, then the exit was going to have to be managed. Our management committee meeting in January 2004 was held at the home of Mike Wells, the club chairman. The key issues were what we were going to do with the two buildings. We had the club premises and our adventure centre in South Wales. Our major concerns were over the risks of the club premises in Winford Grove. It was in a poor state of repair and would raise significant health and safety issues if left unoccupied. Young Bristol had a representative on the club's management committee and in those days it was Lee Williams. The decision was taken to sell the club's adventure centre and use the money to demolish the club's premises leaving the site safe. The decision was unanimous.

What happened next can only be described as bizarre. We received a letter from Young Bristol advising they had reported us to the Charity Commission for the proposed disposal and destruction of charitable assets – even though they had been represented at the management committee meeting that had agreed the decision. From my perspective, it was clear that they had an alternative agenda – I just wasn't sure what it was at that point. Tensions between us and Young Bristol were high, following their letter However, on the basis that YB were going to take responsibility for the club building, we no longer needed to sell the adventure centre. Tal-y-Sarn had not been used in later years as much as it had previously been. Along with major changes in kids' attitudes came a lack of interest in residential activities. We were now in the world of computer-generated entertainment solutions – spending the night in a sleeping bag on an old railway line didn't have the same appeal.

During the early years at Winford Grove, we had a formed an alliance with some of the traditional boys' clubs in the city – two, in particular: Bristol 5 Boys' Club, which had been run by Brian Bennett, and Manor Farm Boys Club which had been run by John Wathen. There was a strong alliance between the boys' clubs of those days and some rivalry. Steve was good friends with the likes of Brian Bennett and Ken Price, who ran Speedwell Boys' Club. John Wathen had been a product of the developing relationship at junior club level, which was run by Dave Phillips. John had started out at St Martin's Boys' Club, which was an annexe of St Martin's Church in Knowle, before moving to Manor Farm. Our biggest rivalry was with Hartcliffe Boys' Club, which was under the leadership of Ernie Curtis. Ernie was a great character and dedicated his whole life to the service of young people. By the time we had come to the pending closure of BDBC, most of these other organisations had either closed completely or had succumbed to the pressure of going mixed in an attempt to maintain their grant-aided status. One club that hadn't was Manor Farm and as a consequence, the management committee made the decision to gift them our adventure centre in South Wales. It did require some work to be undertaken on it and Manor Farm would have to find the funds to do that (which they did) but the building itself was sound. But at least the premises that had brought so much pleasure to the members of Bedminster Down Boys' Club would now benefit the members of a boys' club with broadly the same ethos. Bob Plumb would have approved, I'm sure.

The exit strategy had been agreed, and we had enough money to last until June 2004. The club's management committee met on 29 January. The attendees were myself, Dave

Scarborough, Mike Wells, Daphne Evans, Ian Hensleigh, Mark 'Pickle' Williams and Trevor Jones from Young Bristol. The atmosphere was tense. An agreement was reached to release the funds held in what were originally restricted club accounts to keep us running as long as possible. Because of the club's financial position, the post of club leader would have to be made redundant, and Russ would be informed in writing, giving him three months' notice. On the 1 February 2004, we issued a statement to the members that Bedminster Down Boys' Club would close its doors forever on Wednesday 16 June of that year.

With Mike Wells unwell, I had taken on the role of the club's chairman. I was still heading up the very small team of voluntary staff that were running the club since November the previous year. It was going to be a very busy time. Throughout this time, Dave, or Scarby, was my ally – as he had always been. More than the club's treasurer, he was a sounding-board, a restraint, an advisor and a friend. He was BDBC through and through. He managed the dwindling funds, ensuring that there would be no outstanding creditors when we left. More importantly, he completely handled the transfer of the deeds of Tal-y-Sarn to Manor Farm, dealt with the Charity Commission and, as far as possible, kept Young Bristol off our backs. Not an easy job when you are an employee of that organisation for two days a week. All I can say is that Dave was born with a great more patience and, indeed, tact than me – so it's just as well he was dealing with YB. In true BDBC style, if we were going to go out then we would go out with style. The Final Dinner was organised for Friday 4 June at Redwood Lodge, Hotel & Country Club.

Of course, the announcement of the club's closure resulted in a significant level of media interest and the normal rhetoric that would follow it. There were interviews, radio, press and TV visits. Probably the saddest thing of all is that many of those who had so much comment to make about the club had little understanding of the organisation itself.

We held the final dinner as planned and they travelled from afar to join us. Not only from across the United Kingdom but from Europe as well – Germany and Denmark for instance. There were speeches, a time to reflect on friends no longer with us, and tears. In somewhat bizarre circumstances, Russ Cooper attended. Despite being suspended from his duties while the police continued their investigations, he decided he would attend – it wouldn't be appropriate for me to comment on that decision, only to say that Russ did what Russ wanted and it wasn't our position to refuse him entry. It was a special evening, superb in true BDBC tradition. Many of the great characters that had blessed the club with their presence over the years came. They mingled with the young adults that had sacrificed so much over the last few months and some of the current membership. Tributes were paid to the pioneers of the 1960s, those that had worked to create the new building in Winford Grove and to those who had supported the organisation until the end. There will be those that say that the focus that night was on the Steve Long era – and I understand that. It wasn't meant to be, it wasn't planned that way. I have the absolute respect for the young volunteers that served the club under Russ Cooper. Unfortunately, I think it will always be the case that history will show that many members will find themselves part of two distinct periods – there were very few people that transcended both eras. For many of us, the celebration that night was about our love for the organisation – the club that bonded us all together.

Some twelve days later on the 16 June 2004, the club opened its doors for the last time. At 9pm I read a short statement to those who were in attendance, members, staff and old boys.

It was after I had read the statement that Pickle had spoken to me – and by doing so, brought me back from my dreams. I had been reminiscing. My mind had rolled quickly over the years that had gone before. Images of Miffer banging out endless tunes on the club's record player or seeing him rolling down Miffer's Hill at Velvet Bottom, Cheddar where we used to go for Whitsun Camp. Open nights, shows and the hubbub of a packed club night – over 100 members filling the premises with their sound of laughter or cries of derision when something didn't go as planned. The smell of cooking from the summer cafe we ran before motorways provided a faster route to Devon and Cornwall from north of the city. The characters that had become part of the club's folklore, stories about individuals that would be retold and retold again – every time something added, fact or fiction. There were those that made good and some that didn't. There are those whose time at the club is deeply embedded in their soul. It is part of who they are now and who they will always be.

Thousands of individuals passed through the front doors over the years, each possibly has a story. On that night, I stood with the young men who had given a huge part of their lives to this organisation. They, like me, had joined as members and made the same journey. Tonight was when the journey would end for us all.

The rest, as they say, is history. We locked the doors for the last time at 10pm, and left – taking our memories with us.

At 4pm on Friday 2 July, I arranged to hand over the keys to YB's representative, Trevor Jones at the club. When I arrived at the premises I was surprised to find that he was accompanied with two people from the local girls' club. They were Goretta Thorne (or Gor as many of us know her), the leader of The Grove, as it had become, and Jane Vowles, a member of their management committee. I was seething. In simple terms YB had arranged for our neighbours to take possession of the premises. It was embarrassing for both Gor and Jane – and out of respect to me they immediately retreated. Did they conspire against us? Of course not (although I did have reservations at the time). They were innocent victims of the circumstances they had been put in. Some ten years later, they are still in their own building and fighting for financial survival themselves.

YB promised the community much. Originally they would be re-opening within twelve months. And then, in March 2005, they announced that the club may have to be pulled down and rebuilt before it could re-open. Now, there's a surprise. They actually paid somebody to tell them what we had told them years earlier. They had reported us to Charity Commission for the proposed destruction of charitable assets and they were actually going to do it themselves. They did pull it down – and it remains to this day as an eyesore to the community. Where a once vibrant boys' club stood, serving the community that loved it for over sixty years, is now wasteland.

I look back to my time at BDBC and have so much to be thankful for. I accept, looking back, that there were missed opportunities – whether they would have changed the end result I am not so sure. Any youth provision must be relevant to the young people it serves. A single sexed organisation was very much the post-war requirement and worked well throughout the 60s, 70s, and even into the 80s. Young people of today have very different needs. Physical activities have been replaced with technology; the love of the outdoors has been replaced by the sanctuary of a bedroom and isolation. As we found out in the latter years of the club, many young people were not interested in responsibility. You can't force democracy on anyone. Saying "you have the responsibility" doesn't make people responsible – they have to want that responsibility. Somewhere along the club's journey everything changed.

For me I look back with pride on what I was part of. I met some incredible people along the way and shared some incredible experiences. I have made friendships that have lasted for over forty years and will last for another forty. I have learned so much about myself and led a fuller life because of it – it has made me the person I am.

You can't change history – it is what it is. This is my view on it, on my time at Bedminster Down Boys' Club. All of us, no matter in what capacity, who were part of it are part of its history in equal measure.